AS Economics
UNIT 1
2ND EDITION

AQA

Module 1: Markets and Market Failure

Ray Powell

To my children, James, Elizabeth and Tom

Philip Allan Updates
Market Place
Deddington
Oxfordshire
OX15 0SE

tel: 01869 338652
fax: 01869 337590
e-mail: sales@philipallan.co.uk
www.philipallan.co.uk

© Philip Allan Updates 2001
First printed January 2001
This edition © Philip Allan Updates 2002

ISBN 0 86003 918 8

This Guide has been written specifically to support students preparing for the AQA AS Economics Unit 1 examination. The content has been neither approved nor endorsed by AQA and remains the sole responsibility of the author.

Printed by Information Press, Eynsham, Oxford

P00099

Contents

Introduction

■ ■ ■

Content Guidance

■ ■ ■

Questions and Answers

Introduction

The aim of this guide is to prepare students for the AQA Advanced Subsidiary Unit 1 examination assessing Module 1: Markets and Market Failure. You should use the guide as follows:

(1) Read the introduction.

(2) The second and third sections of the book should then be used as supplements to other resources, such as class notes, textbooks, *Economic Review* magazine and *AS/A-Level Economics Exam Revision Notes.* (The last two of these are published by Philip Allan Updates.) Because it contains summaries rather than in-depth coverage of all the topics in the specification, you should not use the guide as your sole learning resource during the main part of the course. However, you may well decide to use it as the key resource in your revision programme. You are strongly advised to make full use of the Question and Answer section, especially in the revision period when you should be concentrating on improving your examination skills.

Examinable skills

The Unit examination is 1 hour long, has a maximum mark of 40 and contains two sections, ECN1/1 and ECN1/2, both of which must be answered. ECN1/1, which accounts for 15 marks (approximately 37% of the total), comprises 15 compulsory **objective test questions**, which in this guide are called multiple-choice questions (MCQs). One mark will be awarded for each MCQ answered correctly. ECN1/2 accounts for 25 marks (approximately 63% of the total) and comprises two **data–response questions** (DRQs), of which you should answer one.

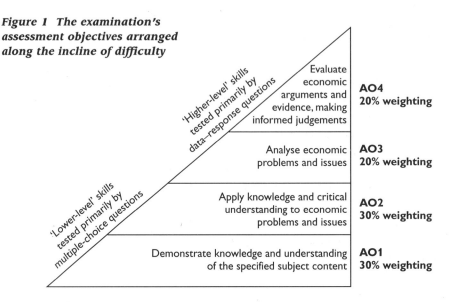

Figure 1 The examination's assessment objectives arranged along the incline of difficulty

'Higher-level' skills tested primarily by data–response questions

Evaluate economic arguments and evidence, making informed judgements — **AO4** **20% weighting**

Analyse economic problems and issues — **AO3** **20% weighting**

'Lower-level' skills tested primarily by multiple-choice questions

Apply knowledge and critical understanding to economic problems and issues — **AO2** **30% weighting**

Demonstrate knowledge and understanding of the specified subject content — **AO1** **30% weighting**

The examination has four **assessment objectives** (AOs), as shown in Figure 1, together with their examination weightings, arranged in an incline of difficulty. 'Lower-level' skills of knowledge and factual recall are included in AO1 (at the bottom of the incline). Moving up the incline, increasingly 'higher-level' skills feature in the AOs: application of knowledge and critical understanding (AO2); analysis of problems (AO3); and evaluation of arguments and evidence (AO4). Overall, 60% of the examination questions are knowledge-based, testing the relatively 'lower-level' skills in AOs 1 and 2. The remaining 40% of examination questions meet AOs 3 and 4.

Multiple-choice skills

Each multiple-choice question contains a 'stem' followed by four possible answers (A, B, C and D), only one of which is correct. Typically, MCQs are set to test candidates' ability to perform simple calculations and their knowledge of key definitions and concepts, especially on parts of the specification not covered by the data–response questions. MCQs primarily test the 'lower-level' skills related to knowledge and under-standing in AOs 1 and 2. You should expect six of the 15 MCQs to test AO1, a further five to test AO2 and the remaining four to test AO3, the analysis of economic problems and issues. AO4 is *not* tested in the multiple-choice question section of the examination paper.

Data–response skills

Whereas the 15 MCQs in the first section of the examination paper are compulsory, the second section comprises two data–response questions of which you must answer one. The DRQs are numbered **Question 1** and **2**. Each question contains three sub-questions, listed as (a), (b) and (c). The mark allocation is (a) 4 marks, (b) 6 marks, (c) 15 marks.

The layout and structure of the questions will be similar to the six data–response questions included in the Question and Answer section of this guide. Each question is likely to contain two or three sets of data, usually extracted from different original sources, such as newspaper or magazine articles. When, for example, three data sets are used in both questions, they will be labelled **Extract A**, **Extract B** and **Extract C** for Question 1, and **Extract D**, **Extract E** and **Extract F** for Question 2. In each question, one set of data is likely to be numerical, for example a line graph, a bar graph, a pie graph or a table. Text or passage data will usually be extracted or adapted from original sources, with the original source indicated. Numerical data will *generally* be taken from original sources, but there may be exceptions. (DRQs 2 and 3 in this guide provide examples, using numerical data in the form of a supply and demand diagram and a production possibility frontier.)

Both DRQs will be structured in exactly the same way and test the same assessment objectives. The questions are supposed to be equally difficult, but in practice almost every student finds one question more attractive than the other. Whichever question you initially favour, don't rush your choice of question. Careful thought and a sensible final decision are necessary if you are to do yourself full justice. You don't want to realise 10 minutes into your answer that you can't answer part (c) and that it is too late to switch questions.

An 'incline of difficulty' will always be built into the DRQs, with the earlier parts of each question being the most straightforward. The first two parts of each DRQ will be marked using an **issue-based mark scheme** which lists the marks that can be awarded for the particular issues (and associated development) that might be included in the answer.

The last part of each DRQ differs from the earlier parts in three significant ways. First, and most obviously, the last part of the question carries many more marks than the earlier three parts — 60% of the total marks for the question and 37% of the total marks for the whole paper. If you time the examination incorrectly and fail to develop your answer to part (c) beyond a cursory footnote, you will reduce considerably your chance of achieving a grade A. Second, whereas questions (a) and (b) should be answered quite briefly, you are expected to write an extended answer of several paragraphs for part (c). You should think of this as a 'mini' essay. Third, 'higher-level' skills are expected. Because of this, a completely different type of mark scheme, known as a **levels of response mark scheme**, is used for the last part of each DRQ. It is vital for you to familiarise yourself with this mark scheme and to bear it in mind when you practise data–response questions.

The first two parts of each DRQ test primarily the 'lower-level' skills of AOs 1 and 2, whereas part (c) tests primarily the 'higher-level' skills set out in AOs 3 and 4. Part (a) of each question will probably relate to the numerical data. You are likely to be asked to describe the main changes in the data, or to compare the changes in two data series.

The second part of each DRQ, (b), is likely to include the key instruction to 'explain'. This question is about the causes of events taking place in the data. It tests whether you can use basic economic theory and analysis in a clear and reasoned way to cast light on an issue. When answering such a question, a 'golden rule' is: *simple theories used well are always preferable to convoluted and difficult theoretical explanations obviously misunderstood.* When the data in the question concern a market (e.g. the oil market), expect the following instruction: 'With the help of a supply and demand diagram, explain...' But even if the question does not contain an explicit instruction to include a diagram, *relevant and accurate* diagrams could improve your answer.

Because part (c) carries significantly more marks it requires a longer and more developed answer than parts (a) and (b). Whereas the earlier parts of the question are firmly based on describing and explaining elements of the data, you should expect part (c) to 'veer away from the data'. The general form that you should expect a part (c) question to take is as follows:

Discuss the possible effects on (some aspect of the wider economy, such as a related market) of (one or more of the events described in the data).

Most importantly, the instruction to '**discuss**' must be obeyed for your answer to reach the higher Level 3 and Level 4 standards of attainment set out in the levels of response mark scheme. Part (c) is the only part of the whole examination paper set specifically to meet assessment objective 4: *evaluation of arguments and evidence*, and the *making of informed judgements*. Your discussion *must* **evaluate** the different arguments you set out in your answer to part (c). With many questions, discussion should centre on **evaluating the advantages and disadvantages** of, the **costs and benefits** of, or the '**case for**' **versus the** '**case against**' pursuing a course of action mentioned in the question.

Finally, always try to finish your answer with a conclusion, the nature of which should vary according to the type of discussion required. The conclusion might judge the relative strengths of the arguments discussed, possibly highlighting the most important argument. With many questions it is more appropriate to conclude whether, on balance, the 'case for' is stronger than the 'case against' and to provide some justification for your opinion.

Even if your conclusion sits on the fence, saying little more than 'it all depends on circumstances', it can earn marks in two different ways. First, a conclusion that justifies your opinion provides the examiner marking your script with evidence of evaluation — the skill needed for your answer to reach a Level 4 or 5 standard. Second, the mark band descriptors that are used for assessing part (c) of each DRQ incorporate statements that relate to the quality of written communication in your answer. To earn maximum marks for this, your answer to part (c) must be well organised and this requires a suitable conclusion.

The mark scheme also instructs the examiner marking your paper to assess the quality of written communication when applying the issue-based mark scheme to parts (a) and (b) of your answer. When deciding how many marks to award for the development of any point made, the examiner must take account of:
- use of appropriate format and style of writing to organise relevant information clearly and coherently
- use of specialist vocabulary, where appropriate
- legibility of handwriting
- accuracy of spelling, punctuation and grammar

A strategy for tackling the examination

(**1**) On opening the examination booklet, turn immediately to the second section and spend up to 5 minutes reading *both* DRQs.

(**2**) Then go back to the first section and spend up to 15 minutes answering the 15 MCQs, completing your first run through the questions. While you are doing this, you will be subconsciously thinking about the DRQs.

(**3**) Read through both DRQs again, paying particular attention to whether you can write a good answer to part (c) of each question, the part that carries the most marks.

(4) After careful thought, make your final choice and spend about 35 minutes answering *all* the parts of the DRQ. Take account of the marks indicated in brackets for each sub-question when allocating the 35 minutes between each part of the question. Make sure you spend over half the time answering part (c).

(5) In the last 5 minutes of the examination, complete a second run through the MCQs and read through your written answers to check for and correct mistakes — including spelling and grammatical mistakes.

Revision planning

Once you have completed your course of study, the most daunting task still remains to be faced: to do yourself justice when presented with unseen questions amid the stresses and strains of the examination room.

If you have studied diligently and if you use this guide wisely, particularly in the weeks leading up to the examination, you should achieve the grade of which you are capable. You can reduce the need for 'luck' by preparing and then following a revision programme. Begin your revision planning several weeks before the examination, timetabling periods of each day when you know you can work for at least an hour completely free of distraction. Allow yourself a brief relaxation period every half-hour or so to facilitate the absorption of what you have revised intensively in the previous period. Although you must cover the whole specification (to enable you to answer all the MCQs), concentrate on key concepts and essential economic theory rather than on descriptive fact and historical detail.

The revision strategy below is based on the use of this guide, supplemented by other resources, such as the notes you have built up over your course of study and favoured textbooks. The programme is designed for the 3-week period before the examination. The strategy assumes you are revising at least three other AS subjects during the same 3-week period, but are able to devote a session of 2 hours (plus half an hour for short breaks) to economics every other day, with shorter 'follow-up' sessions on the intervening days. You should revise solidly for 6 days a week, but allow yourself 1 day off a week to recharge your batteries. The strategy can be modified to meet your personal needs and preferences: for example, by shortening each revision session and/or extending the sessions over a revision period longer than 3 weeks.

(1) Revise one topic from the Content Guidance section of this guide per revision session. Divide the revision session into four half-hour periods, during which you are working solidly and without distraction, interspersed with 10-minute breaks.

(2) Proceed through the topics in the order they appear in the guide:
Week 1: 1–3
Week 2: 4–6
Week 3: 7–9

(3) Vary the activities you undertake in each 30-minute period of a revision session. For example, spend the first 30 minutes reading through the 'Essential information' section of the topic. List key terms and concepts on a piece of paper. After a short break, use the second 30-minute period to check more fully the meaning of the key terms and concepts in your class notes and/or an economics textbook. Then, after a second short break, check which multiple-choice questions and parts of data–response questions in the Question and Answer section of the guide test aspects of the topic you are revising. Spend the rest of the 30 minutes answering some or all of the questions. In the final 30-minute period (or perhaps in a 'follow-up' session a day or two later), carefully read through the examiner's comments on the MCQs and the student's answers and examiner's comments on the DRQs covered by the topic.

(4) To vary your revision programme, and to make sure you reinforce and retain the vital information revised in the longer sessions, fit some of the activities suggested below into follow-up sessions. Normally you should plan at least a single half-hour 'follow-up' session for each day between your 'long session' days. Be prepared also to undertake unplanned 10-minute sessions whenever you find yourself with a few spare minutes — for example, when waiting for a meal or for a television programme to start. Activities suitable for follow-up and 10-minute sessions include the following:

- **Write definitions** of some the key terms and concepts relating to the topic revised on the previous day. Check each of your definitions against the correct definition in this guide, in a textbook or in your class notes.
- **Draw** key diagrams relating to the topic. Check any diagram you draw against a correct version of the diagram, making absolutely sure that the diagram is correctly and clearly labelled.
- Whenever you make mistakes, **repeat these exercises** every day or so, until you have eliminated all the mistakes.
- **Answer questions** from past AQA examination papers and from AQA's 'Specimen Units and Mark Schemes' booklet, which your teacher should have. Make sure your teacher obtains all the relevant AQA past exam papers that are available at the time you take the examination. Identify and then answer questions from past papers that relate to the topic just revised. Then spend another follow-up session checking your answer(s) against the AQA mark scheme(s) to see how you could improve.

Note: if you wish to buy copies of past examination papers and mark schemes, contact: The Publications Department, The Assessment and Qualifications Alliance, Aldon House, 39 Heald Grove, Manchester M14 4NA (tel: 0161 953 1170).

Content
Guidance

Economics can be divided into two broad areas of study: **macroeconomics** and **microeconomics**. Macroeconomics (which looks at how the economy functions as a whole) is the subject matter of Module 2: The National Economy. By contrast, Module 1: Markets and Market Failure is concerned solely with microeconomics — the study of individual **markets** within the economy, and the economic behaviour of individual **consumers** (or **households**) and **firms** (or **producers**) in such markets.

As the title of the module indicates, the specification (or syllabus) requires you to study two rather different aspects of microeconomics: the circumstances in which markets perform well and the circumstances in which markets perform badly. Any circumstance in which a market performs badly is called a **market failure**.

The introduction to this section of the guide (pp. 13–15) contains a summary of the AQA specification for Module 1: Markets and Market Failure. This is followed by more detail about each section of the specification under the following headings:
- The economic problem (p. 16)
- Supply and demand in competitive markets (p. 18)
- Elasticity (p. 21)
- Prices and resource allocation (p. 25)
- Monopolies and resource allocation (p. 27)
- Production and efficiency (p. 30)
- Public goods and externalities (p. 33)
- Merit and demerit goods, and inequalities in the distributions of income and wealth (p. 36)
- Governments and markets (p. 39)

Introduction to the specification

The AQA specification for Markets and Market Failure contains the following sections.

10.1 The economic problem

How can you decide whether a market performs well or badly? You must assess the extent to which the market contributes to the solution of the **economic problem**, which is the title of both the first section of the specification and the first topic in this guide. A market performs well when the **price mechanism**, operating within the market, solves to a satisfactory degree the economic problem of **scarcity**. By contrast, if the price mechanism (or market mechanism) functions unsatisfactorily (or, in extreme cases, breaks down completely and fails to function at all), **market failure** occurs.

The key concepts you must know which relate to the economic problem of scarcity are: the nature of **economic resources** or **factors of production**; the importance of **choice**, **opportunity cost** and the concept of the **margin**; and the assumption that all **economic agents** (households, firms and the government) have **objectives** that they wish to maximise. **Production possibility curve** diagrams (which also figure in specification section 10.5 in relation to the key concept of economic efficiency) can be used to illustrate the economic problem and two other key concepts in section 10.1: **opportunity cost** and the **trade-off** between conflicting objectives. Finally, this section of the specification requires that you recognise **value judgements** and understand the difference between **positive statements** (statements of fact or statements that can be shown to be either true or false) and **normative statements** (statements of opinion).

10.2 The allocation of resources in competitive markets

This is the core area of the specification, at the centre of which is the **supply and demand economic model**. To meet the requirements of this section of the specification, you must learn, understand and be able to apply important terms and concepts such as **demand, supply, equilibrium, disequilibrium, elasticity**, and the **signalling, incentive** and **rationing functions of prices**. Make sure you can apply **elasticity formulae** to calculate **price elasticity of demand, income elasticity of demand, cross elasticity of demand** and **price elasticity of supply**. You must understand the difference between a **shift** of a demand or supply curve and an **adjustment** along a supply or demand curve in response to a price change. Practise drawing **supply and demand diagrams** to illustrate shifts of supply and demand caused by changes in **factors, other than price, which determine supply and demand**.

Probably the most important skill you must learn when studying this section of the specification is **applying demand and supply analysis to particular markets**. This is a key skill tested in the Unit 1 examination — one of the two data–response questions is likely to be set on a **primary product or industrial market**. In addition, it is an equally important skill required for answering questions on the **housing, and sport and leisure markets** in the examination for AS Module 3: Markets at Work.

10.3 Monopoly

Whereas section 10.2 assumes that a market is one of many competitive markets in the economy, section 10.3 requires knowledge and understanding of markets where firms possess considerable **market power**. In an extreme case, there will be only one firm in the market — a situation known as **pure monopoly**. You must learn how to apply terms and concepts listed in sections 10.4, 10.5 and 10.6 to the analysis of monopoly. These are **efficiency** and **economies of scale** (10.4); **market failure** and **market imperfections** (10.5); and **government intervention** to correct the market failure associated with monopoly (10.6). You must also learn to draw diagrams to show how, compared to a competitive market, a monopoly can **restrict output** and **force up the price**.

10.4 Production and efficiency

Throughout your studies you must always remember that **improved economic welfare** is the ultimate purpose of economic activity, but that **production** of more goods and services is usually necessary for welfare to increase. In order to maximise welfare, production must take place **efficiently** rather than **inefficiently**. You must understand the difference between **productive efficiency** and **allocative efficiency**. Productive efficiency involves maximising output of goods and services from available inputs (the economic resources or factors of production mentioned in section 10.1). Two factors that increase productive efficiency are **specialisation** and **economies of scale**. Specialisation, which occurs when different industries produce different goods and services, leads to the growth of **trade** and **exchange**. Economies of scale, which result from the growth in size of firms and industries, lead to falling average costs of production. The economy as a whole is productively efficient when it is producing on its **production possibility boundary** or frontier. Allocative efficiency relates to consumption, or the final uses of goods and services. The specification defines allocative efficiency in terms of the goods and services produced matching people's needs and preferences. If markets fail to achieve allocative efficiency, **resource misallocation** and **market failure** result — key concepts in section 10.5.

10.5 Market failure

Market failure occurs whenever markets perform badly or unsatisfactorily. Markets may fail either because they perform **inequitably** (**unfairly** or **unjustly**) or because they perform **inefficiently**. Different people have different opinions on fairness and unfairness, so the first type of market failure depends on **normative** views or value judgements (see section 10.1). Many economists argue that **inequalities in the distributions of income and wealth** provide a significant example of market failure resulting from markets performing inequitably. Whenever markets are productively or allocatively inefficient (key concepts in section 10.4), the second type of market failure occurs. **Monopoly**, the subject of section 10.3, is an important example. If the **incentive function of prices** (see section 10.2) breaks down completely, markets may be unable to produce any quantity of a good. **Public goods** provide the main example, and there are also **'missing markets'** in **externalities**. In other cases, markets may succeed in providing a good, but end up providing an allocatively inefficient quantity. The main examples are **merit** and **demerit goods**.

10.6 Government intervention in the market

When studying government intervention, you should distinguish between the government's **objectives** and the **methods** it uses to achieve its objectives. Section 10.1 introduced one of the most important assumptions in economics — that every economic agent has an objective that it tries to achieve and maximise. When analysing the role of the state in the economy, economists usually assume that governments wish to **maximise the public interest** or **social welfare** (i.e. the economic welfare of the whole community).

When intervening in the market, governments have various **policy instruments** at their disposal. The most extreme method of intervention involves **abolishing the market**, as when the government **provides public and merit goods directly** and finances their provision through the tax system. At the other extreme, governments often allow markets to function largely free of intervention, but modified to some extent by the effect of taxes or minor regulation. **Taxation** and **regulation** provide the main forms of government intervention in markets. Other methods of intervention cited in the specification include **subsidies**, **price controls** and in the case of negative externalities, **permits to pollute**. You might also be asked to explain, analyse and assess the effectiveness of intervention in the form of **buffer stock schemes** or **price stabilisation policies**, although such policies are not mentioned explicitly in the specification. The specification hints that the **Common Agricultural Policy (CAP)** of the European Union may provide the context for a question on government intervention in agricultural markets. Government intervention in the **transport market** might also figure strongly in a question.

Much government intervention attempts to correct the various **market failures** outlined in section 10.5. However, an attempt to correct market failure can lead to **government failure**. First, government intervention to correct a market failure or to achieve the government's objectives may simply be unsuccessful. Second, and often more seriously, completely new economic problems may emerge as a direct result of government intervention trying to correct other problems.

The economic problem

These notes relate to AQA specification section 10.1 and prepare you to answer examination questions on the following:

- the purpose of economic activity
- the fundamental economic problem of scarcity
- related economic concepts, such as opportunity cost and the conflicts or trade-offs involved when economic agents try to achieve their goals or objectives

Essential information

Economics is literally the study of economising — the study of how human beings make choices on **what to produce**, **how to produce** and **for whom to produce**, in a world in which most of the resources are limited. Because resources are limited in relation to people's infinite wants, the problem of **scarcity** is the **fundamental economic problem**.

The ultimate purpose or **objective of economic activity** is to increase people's happiness or **economic welfare**. Increased **production** enables economic welfare to increase, but only if the production of more goods and services leads to higher levels of **consumption**. Production and consumption often lead to resource **depletion** (using up scarce resources) and resource **degradation** (e.g. pollution and destruction of the natural environment).

As a general rule, consumption increases **economic welfare** and people's **standard of living** (although in certain circumstances consumption can reduce rather than increase welfare). Economists often use the word **utility** for the welfare that people enjoy when they consume goods and services. Goods such as food bought for consumption are known as **consumer goods**; by contrast, a good such as a machine bought by a firm in order to produce other goods is called a **capital good**. Goods that people produce for their own consumption, and activities such as contemplating the natural environment, contribute to people's utility or welfare, adding to the utility obtained from consuming goods bought in the **market**.

The **production possibility frontier** in Figure 1 shows the various possible combinations of capital goods and consumer goods that the economy can produce when all the available inputs or economic resources are being used to the full.

Suppose that initially the economy is at point A on the frontier, producing K_1 capital goods and C_1 consumer goods. In the absence of **economic growth** (which moves the frontier outwards), consumer good production can only increase to C_2 if the production of capital goods falls from to K_1 to K_2. In the technical jargon of economics, the **opportunity cost** of increasing output of consumer goods is the alternative output, in this case capital goods, sacrificed or forgone.

content guidance

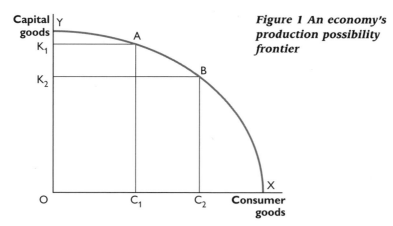

Figure 1 An economy's production possibility frontier

Economists usually assume that **households** and **firms** (and other **economic agents**, such as the **government**) have economic **objectives** that they wish to **maximise**. The objectives are generally taken to be **profit** in the case of **producers** (or firms) and **utility** for **consumers** (or households). Economic behaviour is thus **maximising behaviour**. (Governments are also assumed to have an objective that they wish to maximise, namely the **public interest**. This is alternatively known as **social welfare**, or the welfare of the whole community.) Everybody is assumed to be **rational**, which means that people always try to choose the best possible outcome in preference to the next best. Hence the opportunity cost of any choice is often defined as 'the next best alternative forgone'. Very often it is difficult to choose between different outcomes that all have advantages and disadvantages. In this situation, it may be possible to resolve the conflict by **trading-off** between the alternatives. Points A and B in Figure 1 illustrate trading-off. Instead of producing *only* capital goods (at point Y) or *only* consumer goods (at point X), combinations of capital *and* consumer goods can be produced at intermediate points on the frontier, such as A or B. The production of capital goods can be *traded-off* against the production of consumer goods.

The concept of the **margin** is also very important when analysing how economic agents seek to maximise welfare and achieve their desired objectives. Suppose you decide to eat five plums. Your total consumption is five, but the fifth plum is the marginal unit consumed. The marginal unit is always the *last* one chosen: the *last* good produced, the *last* hour worked etc. Relating back to the production possibility frontier, a **marginal increase** in consumer good production must involve a **marginal fall** in capital good production, provided that the economy is initially on the frontier.

Examination skills

The skills most likely to be tested by multiple-choice and data–response questions on the economic problem are as follows:
- Interpreting and possibly drawing a production possibility diagram such as Figure 1.
- Understanding and explaining that the purpose of economic activity is to increase welfare.

- Understanding and explaining how the scenario of the question illustrates the problem of scarcity.
- Explaining and applying the concept of opportunity cost.
- Analysing an economic problem in terms of trade-offs between conflicting objectives.
- Distinguishing between a statement of fact (a positive statement) and a value judgement (a normative statement).

Examination questions

Because it is *the* central topic in economics, virtually every examination question in economics touches upon the economic problem and its related concepts. For the most part, specific knowledge of the economic problem will be tested by multiple-choice questions rather than by data–response questions. You should expect up to two multiple-choice questions on the terms and concepts listed in specification section 10.1. In the Question and Answer section of this guide, MCQs 1 and 2 in both Tests 1 and 2 provide typical examples. You should answer these questions either now or in your revision programme, and then carefully read the examiner's comments for each question. DRQ 3 also focuses strongly on the economic problem. The question tests your ability to interpret a production possibility diagram, together with your knowledge of the problem of scarcity and opportunity cost.

Common examination errors

Commonly made mistakes on the economic problem include the following:
- Failure to appreciate that almost all problems and issues in economics involve the problem of scarcity and its related concepts.
- Failure to relate scarcity to the need for rationing, and to the role of rationing mechanisms such as the price mechanism and queues and waiting lists.
- Inaccurate drawing of production possibility diagrams.
- Not understanding the importance of the assumption of maximising behaviour in economic theory.
- Confusing positive and normative statements (see the examiner's comment on MCQ 1 in Test 1 for a full explanation of the difference).

Supply and demand in competitive markets

These notes relate to AQA specification section 10.2 and prepare you to answer examination questions on the following:
- how the price mechanism establishes an equilibrium within a market
- how the market adjusts to a new equilibrium following a shift of demand or supply

content guidance

Essential information

A **market**, which is a meeting of buyers and sellers for the purpose of exchanging goods or services, exists in the market sector of the economy. Figure 2 illustrates the key features of a market.

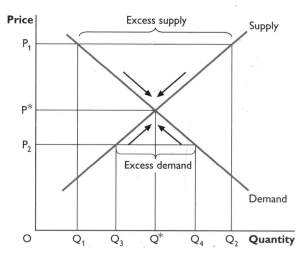

Figure 2 The price mechanism operating within a market

The **demand curve** shows the quantities of a good that households or consumers *plan* to purchase at different prices, and the **supply curve** shows how much firms or producers *plan* to supply at different prices. At all prices (except the **equilibrium price**) it is impossible for both households and firms simultaneously to fulfil their market plans. For example, at price P_1 firms would like to supply Q_2, but households are only willing to purchase Q_1. **Planned supply** is greater than **planned demand**, resulting in an **excess supply**. By contrast, at price P_2 households wish to buy Q_4 but firms restrict supply to Q_3, and **excess demand** results. At any price other than P^*, which is the equilibrium price, there will be either excess supply or excess demand, with either the firms or the households unable to fulfil their market plans. The market is in **disequilibrium** when there is excess supply or demand.

In economics, we assume that firms respond to excess supply by reducing the price they are prepared to accept, while conversely households bid up the price to eliminate excess demand. The price falls or rises until equilibrium is achieved. The equilibrium price is the only price that satisfies both households and firms, which consequently have no reason to change their market plans. At P^* planned demand = planned supply.

Market equilibrium may be disturbed by a **shift** of either the demand curve or the supply curve. A demand curve will shift if any of the factors influencing demand, *other than the good's own price*, changes. These factors, which are sometimes called the **conditions of demand**, include income, tastes and preferences, and the prices of **substitute goods** and **goods in joint demand**. An increase in income shifts demand curves rightwards — but only for **normal goods**. A normal good is defined as a good for which demand increases when income increases. By contrast, an **inferior good** is a good (such as poor-quality food) for which demand falls as income increases. If the good is inferior, an increase in income shifts the demand curve leftwards. Figure 3 shows a rightward shift of demand from D_1 to D_2, caused perhaps by a fall in the price of a good in joint demand (a **complementary good**) or by a successful advertising campaign for the product. Before the shift of demand, P_1 was an equilibrium price. Following the shift of demand, this is no longer the case. Planned demand is greater than planned supply and there is excess demand of $Q_2 - Q_1$ in the market. To relieve the excess demand, the price rises to a new equilibrium at P_2.

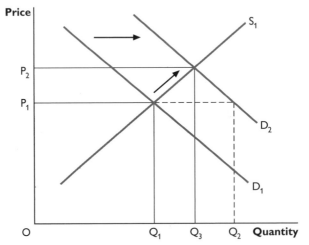

Figure 3
The effect of a rightward shift of demand in a market

By contrast, if **conditions of supply** change, the supply curve shifts. The conditions of supply include costs of production and taxes levied upon firms by government. For example, an increase in labour costs would shift the supply curve upwards (or leftwards).

Examination skills

The skills most likely to be tested by multiple-choice and data–response questions on supply and demand in competitive markets are as follows:
- Interpreting a graph or table to describe the changes taking place over a period of time in the price of a good.
- Interpreting a graph or table to compare changes in the prices of two goods.
- Drawing a supply and demand diagram to illustrate the market in equilibrium.
- Identifying a change in *either* the conditions of demand *or* the conditions of supply, and the resulting shift of either the demand curve or the supply curve.
- Explaining how the market mechanism operates to eliminate excess demand or excess supply, and the adjustment of the market to a new equilibrium.

- Distinguishing between a shift of a demand or supply curve, and an adjustment in response to a price change along a demand or supply curve.
- Analysing goods in joint demand (complementary goods, such as cars and petrol), competing demand (substitute goods, such as tea and coffee) and joint supply (such as beef and leather).

Examination questions

You should expect about two multiple-choice questions on supply and demand in competitive markets. See MCQs 3 and 4 in Test 1 and MCQ 2 in Test 2 for examples. The topic is also likely to figure prominently in at least one of the two optional data–response questions. The AQA specification states that 'commodity markets (including the oil market), agriculture, transport and the market for health care provide examples of contexts within which questions will often be set'. The health care market, which figured in AQA's specimen exam paper, appeared in the June 2002 exam, so oil, the other specimen topic, may also figure in a future exam.

Markets for primary products are likely to figure prominently in data–response questions set on supply and demand in competitive markets. Expect the question to focus on a particular market, such as the silver market or the market for an agricultural commodity such as cotton or tea. Questions may also be set on industrial markets for manufactured goods, such as cars or compact discs.

Common examination errors

Commonly made mistakes on supply and demand in competitive markets include the following:
- Confusing a shift of a demand curve with an adjustment along a demand curve (likewise, confusing a shift of a supply curve with an adjustment along a supply curve).
- Confusing the factors that cause a demand curve to shift with those that cause a supply curve to shift.
- Drawing supply and demand graphs with the curves and axes wrongly labelled.
- Confusing excess demand and excess supply.
- Confusing normal goods and inferior goods when a change in income causes a demand curve to shift.

Elasticity

These notes relate to AQA specification section 10.2 and prepare you to answer examination questions on the following:
- elasticities of demand and supply
- application of appropriate elasticities to explain how particular markets function and to analyse problems of resource allocation in such markets

Essential information

Whenever a change in one variable (such as a good's price) causes a change to occur in a second variable (such as the quantity of the good that firms are prepared to supply), an elasticity can be calculated. The **elasticity** measures the **proportionate responsiveness** of the second variable to the change in the first variable. For example, if a 5% increase in price were to cause firms to increase supply more than proportionately (say, by 10%), supply would be **elastic**. If the response were less than proportionate (for example, an increase in supply of only 3%), supply would be **inelastic**. And if the change in price were to induce an exactly proportionate change in supply, supply would be neither elastic nor inelastic — this is called **unit elasticity of supply**.

The formulae for the four elasticities you need to know are:

(1) Price elasticity of demand $= \dfrac{\text{proportionate change in quantity demanded}}{\text{proportionate change in price}}$

(2) Income elasticity of demand $= \dfrac{\text{proportionate change in quantity demanded}}{\text{proportionate change in income}}$

(3) Cross elasticity of demand for good A with respect to the price of B $= \dfrac{\text{proportionate change in quantity of A demanded}}{\text{proportionate change in price of B}}$

(4) Price elasticity of supply $= \dfrac{\text{proportionate change in quantity supplied}}{\text{proportionate change in price}}$

Price elasticity of demand measures consumers' responsiveness to a change in a good's own price. **Substitutability** is the most important determinant of price elasticity of demand. When a substitute exists for a product, consumers can respond to a price rise by switching expenditure away from the good, buying instead the substitute whose price has not risen. Demand for **necessities** tends to be inelastic as they have few substitutes. Other determinants of price elasticity of demand include the following:

- **Percentage of income:** goods or services upon which households spend a large proportion of their income tend to be in more elastic demand than small items upon which only a fraction of income is spent.
- **The 'width' of the market definition:** the demand for Shell petrol is much more price elastic than the market demand for petrol produced by all the oil companies.
- **Time:** although there are exceptions, demand for many goods and services is more elastic in the long run than in the short run because it takes time to respond to a price change.

Income elasticity of demand — which measures how demand responds to a change in income — is always negative for an **inferior good** and positive for a **normal good**. The quantity demanded of an inferior good falls as income rises, whereas demand for a normal good rises with income. Normal goods are sometimes further subdivided into **superior goods** or **luxuries**, for which the income elasticity of demand is greater than unity, and **basic goods**, with an income elasticity of less than 1.

Cross elasticity of demand measures the responsiveness of demand for one commodity to changes in the price of another good. The cross elasticity of demand between two goods or services indicates the nature of the demand relationship between the goods. There are three possibilities: **joint demand** (negative cross elasticity); **competing demand** or **substitutes** (positive cross elasticity); and an absence of any discernible demand relationship (zero cross elasticity).

Price elasticity of supply measures the extent to which firms are prepared to increase output in response to a change in price. Its main determinants are as follows:

- **Length of the production period:** when firms convert raw materials into finished goods for sale in a production period of just a few hours or days, supply is more elastic than when several months are involved, as in many types of agricultural production.
- **Existence of spare capacity:** when a firm possesses spare capacity and when labour and raw materials are readily available, it is usually possible to increase production quickly in the short run.
- **Ease of accumulating stocks:** when unsold stocks of finished goods can be stored at low cost, firms will be able to meet any sudden increase in demand from stock. Supply also tends to be elastic when firms can quickly increase production by drawing on their stocks of raw materials.
- **Ease of factor substitution:** supply tends to be relatively elastic if firms can use different combinations of labour and capital to produce a particular level of output.
- **Number of firms in the market:** generally the greater the number of firms in the market, the more elastic is market or industry supply.
- **Time:** supply is completely inelastic in the **market period** or **momentary period**, often relatively inelastic in the **short run**, and much more elastic in the **long run** when a firm can change the scale of all its inputs or factors of production in response to a change in demand and price.

Examination skills

The skills most likely to be tested by multiple-choice and data–response questions on elasticity are as follows:

- Calculating an elasticity using the appropriate formula.
- Interpreting the economic meaning and significance of an elasticity.
- Drawing and explaining a diagram illustrating elastic or inelastic demand or supply.
- Explaining events in a market in terms of elasticities of demand and supply.
- Applying elasticity analysis to assess the economic effect of decisions made by firms or consumers.
- Evaluating the effects of government policies such as a decision to increase an indirect tax.

Examination questions

You should expect up to three multiple-choice questions on elasticity. MCQs 7 in Test 1, and 6, 8 and 14 in Test 2 in the Question and Answer section of this guide provide typical examples. Take special note of MCQ 14 in Test 2, which tests understanding of an application of elasticity which many students find difficult. Imposing or raising an indirect tax shifts a good's supply curve upwards, but the effect on price and the incidence of the tax (who bears the tax) depends on the elasticity of the demand curve. More generally, when a supply curve (or a demand curve) shifts, the extent to which price or quantity changes in the process of adjustment to the new equilibrium depends upon the elasticity of the *other curve*, i.e. the curve that does not shift. This very important point is illustrated in the three panels of Figure 4, which show a rightward shift of supply along demand curves of different elasticities.

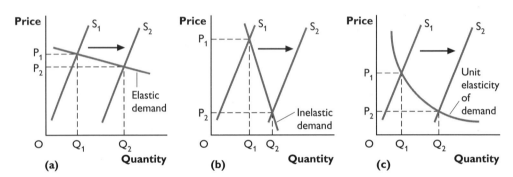

***Figure 4** The extent to which price and quantity change following a shift of supply depends upon price elasticity of demand*

When demand is elastic (Figure 4a), the quantity bought and sold adjusts much more than price. The reverse is true when demand is inelastic (Figure 4b). Finally, when demand is unit elastic (depicted in the rectangular hyperbola in Figure 4c), price and quantity change by equal percentages. Your understanding of this very important point may well be tested by a data–response question.

Common examination errors

Commonly made mistakes on elasticity include the following:
- Confusing elasticity with slope. By definition, straight-line demand and supply curves have constant slopes, but elasticity varies from point to point along many (though not all) demand and supply curves (see MCQ 10).
- Missing out the word 'proportionate' or 'percentage' in elasticity formulae (as in 'proportionate change in quantity demanded').
- Incorrectly writing elasticity formulae 'upside down' (e.g. putting price on the top line and quantity on the bottom line of the formula for price elasticity of demand).
- Writing about the wrong elasticity — particularly about elasticity of *demand* when the question asks about elasticity of *supply*.
- Drifting into 'write all you know' mode, or churning out facts and diagrams for all the elasticities the candidate can think of, without applying knowledge selectively to address the issue posed by the question.

Prices and resource allocation

These notes relate to AQA specification section 10.2 and prepare you to answer examination questions on the following:

- resource allocation in market economies and mixed economies
- the functions that prices perform when allocating scarce resources among competing uses in markets

Essential information

Prices provide the main method through which scarce resources are allocated between competing uses in virtually all modern economies. In a pure **market economy** — made up solely of markets — the price mechanism is the only **allocative mechanism** solving the economic problem (apart from inheritance and other gifts, luck such as winning the lottery, and theft). However, most modern economies, including the UK economy, are not pure market economies. They are **mixed economies**, containing a mix of **private and state ownership** of the **means of production** (**capital**), and a mix of **market and non-market provision** of goods and services, i.e. they have a **market sector** and a **non-market sector**. In the non-market sector, the government uses the **planning mechanism** to provide goods and services such as police, roads and health care. Figure 5 illustrates three different types of **economic system**: planned economies (or command economies), mixed economies and market economies. The price mechanism operates within mixed and market economies, but only to a limited extent (for example, in black markets) in a planned economy (such as the communist economies of eastern Europe before the collapse of communism around 1990).

Figure 5 Planned, mixed and market economies

Within a market economy or the market sector of a mixed economy, three conditions are necessary for a market to operate:

- The individual buyers and sellers decide what, how, how much, where and when to trade or exchange.
- They do so with reference to their self-interest and to the alternatives or opportunities open to them; the exchange must be voluntary; if one party forces a transaction upon the other, it is not a market transaction.
- Prices convey information to buyers and sellers about self-interest and opportunities; for a market to allocate resources among different types of activity and to coordinate economic activity throughout the economy, prices must respond to the forces of supply and demand.

Prices perform three main functions in a market or mixed economy:
- **The signalling function.** Prices signal what is available, conveying the information that allows all the traders in the market to plan and coordinate their economic activities. Markets will function inefficiently, sometimes breaking down completely, leading to **market failure**, if prices signal wrong or misleading information.
- **The incentive function.** Prices create incentives for **economic agents** (e.g. households and firms) to behave and make decisions in ways consistent with pursuing and achieving the fulfilment of their self-interest.
- **The allocative function or rationing function.** For markets to operate in an orderly and efficient manner, the buyers and sellers in the market must respond to the incentives provided by the price mechanism. Suppose that, in a particular market, demand rises relative to supply, causing the market price to rise. An immediate result is that the rising price limits to some extent the increase in the demand for the good or service, which has now become more expensive compared to other goods, thereby creating for consumers an incentive to economise in its use. But simultaneously, the possibility of higher profits creates for firms an incentive to shift resources into producing the goods and services whose relative price has risen and to demand more resources, such as labour and capital, in order to increase production. In turn, this may bid up wages and the price of capital, creating for households and the owners of capital an incentive to switch the supply of labour and capital into industries where the prices of inputs or factors of production are rising. In this way, the changing prices of goods and services relative to each other allocate and ration the economy's scarce resources to the consumers and firms who are willing and able to pay most for them.

Over 200 years ago, the economist Adam Smith described how the **invisible or hidden hand of the market**, operating in competitive markets and through the pursuit of self-interest, achieves an allocation of resources that is also in society's interest. This remains the central view of all **free-market economists**, i.e. those who believe in the virtues of a competitive market economy subject to minimum government intervention.

Examination skills

The skills most likely to be tested by multiple-choice or data–response questions on prices and resource allocation are as follows:
- Identifying and explaining the signalling, incentive creating, and allocative functions of prices.
- Applying knowledge of the functions of prices to a particular market, such as an agricultural market.
- Explaining how the price mechanism functions within a market to eliminate excess supply or demand and achieve equilibrium.
- Explaining how the price mechanism allocates resources among markets as consumers substitute cheaper for more expensive goods, and firms move from less profitable into more profitable markets.
- Evaluating how well or how badly prices perform these functions.

Examination questions

You should expect one multiple-choice question that relates explicitly to the functions of prices. See MCQ 11 in Test 1 for an example. A data–response question might also ask you to identify one or more of the functions of prices in the information about a market contained within the data. For example, an alternative question (c) for DRQ 1 in the Question and Answer section of this guide, which is based on the market for paper pulp, might be: *'Explain how the sustained upward movement in the prices of forestry industry products mentioned in Extract A provides an example of the incentive and allocative functions of prices.'*

Even if a data–response question does not ask explicitly about the signalling, incentive, and allocative functions of prices, relevant application of knowledge of these functions can often earn high marks. This is particularly true of the last part of a data–response question, for which a levels of response marking scheme is used to allocate the 15 marks available. Appropriate application of knowledge of the functions of prices in the task of resource allocation in the economy may well be the key skill that raises the standard of your answer from Level 3 to Level 4 or 5. See, for example, part (c) of DRQ 2, which asks for a discussion of whether consumers benefit from black markets. A good answer might argue that, within a black market, prices perform a useful allocative function, improving on the situation in the main market, where prices send out the wrong signals and result in resource misallocation.

Common examination errors

Commonly made mistakes on prices and resource allocation include the following:
- Failure to understand the decentralised and unorganised nature of a market.
- Inability to relate the functions of prices to the economic problem of scarcity.
- Failure to relate the functions of prices to the pursuit of self-interest, to consumers' utility-maximising objectives and to firms' profit-maximising objectives.
- A lack of appreciation that 'market failure' and resource misallocation occur when prices malfunction.

Monopolies and resource allocation

These notes relate to AQA specification section 10.3 and prepare you to answer examination questions on the following:
- the meaning of monopoly and monopoly power
- whether monopoly leads to resource misallocation or whether there may be circumstances in which the benefits of monopoly exceed the costs

Essential information

Economists use the word **monopoly** in three rather different ways:

- **Pure monopoly** is a market structure in which there is only one firm. Because it is completely protected by **barriers to entry**, the firm faces no competition at all.
- Many firms, even those in quite competitive markets, possess a degree of **monopoly power**. Monopoly power (or **market power**) is the ability to influence the market: for example, by setting a price and using persuasive advertising to get consumers to buy the good. In pure monopoly, but also in highly concentrated markets (markets dominated by just a few firms), firms possess sufficient monopoly power to function as **price makers** rather than as **price takers**.
- Any industry dominated by a few large firms is often loosely called a monopoly, although more accurately it is an example of highly imperfect competition or **oligopoly**.

Monopoly power is strongest when a firm produces an essential good for which there are no substitutes — or when demand is relatively inelastic. **Natural monopoly** occurs when there is room in the market for only one firm benefiting from full **economies of scale**. In the past, **utility industries** such as water, gas, electricity and the telephone industries were natural monopolies. The industries produced a service that was delivered through a distribution network or grid of pipes or cables into millions of separate businesses and homes. Competition in the provision of distribution grids was regarded as wasteful, since it required the duplication of fixed capacity, therefore causing each supplier to incur unnecessarily high fixed costs. In recent years, technical progress, particularly in the telecommunications industry, has weakened and some-times destroyed the natural monopoly status of the utility industries. Nevertheless, the UK government continues to regulate the utility industries to try to prevent the abuse of monopoly power.

Other causes of monopoly are:

- geographical (e.g. a single grocery store in an isolated village)
- government-created monopolies that are protected from competition by the law (e.g. gambling casinos)
- control of market outlets and raw materials (e.g. breweries and oil companies denying competitors access to the pubs and petrol stations they own)
- advertising as a barrier to entry — large firms can prevent small firms entering the market through **saturation advertising**

Figure 6 illustrates how a monopoly may adversely affect resource allocation. In the absence of monopoly, a competitive industry produces output Q_1, which is sold at price P_1. If a monopoly is formed, the firm restricts output to Q_2 and raises the price to P_2, thereby exploiting consumers. Other arguments against monopoly are as follows:

- They restrict consumer choice.
- Because they don't face competition, monopolies incur unnecessarily high costs and are productively inefficient (see p. 32).

- Consumers suffer because **producer sovereignty** replaces **consumer sovereignty** (i.e. the monopoly does not respond to consumers' wishes, preferring instead an 'easy life'). As a result, monopolies are **allocatively inefficient** (see also p. 32).

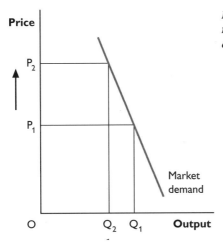

Figure 6 A monopoly restricting output and raising the price

However, under certain circumstances (including natural monopoly), monopoly may be justified. The two main justifications of monopoly are as follows:

- By achieving **economies of scale**, a monopoly can produce at lower average cost and be more productively efficient than smaller firms in a competitive industry.
- A monopoly may be **innovative** because the firm can enjoy the fruits of successful innovation in the form of monopoly profit. By contrast, a competitive firm may lack the incentive to innovate if competitors can instantly copy any successful innovation. This is the justification of **patent legislation**, which gives firms an exclusive right to exploit their innovations for a number of years.

If the benefits of monopoly exceed the costs, monopoly may be condoned. Nevertheless, there is still a case for government intervention to **regulate** the monopoly in order to prevent the firm abusing its market power.

Examination skills

The skills most likely to be tested by multiple-choice or data–response questions on monopolies and resource allocation are as follows:

- Identifying causes of monopoly and monopoly power.
- Applying key theoretical concepts such as efficiency and economies of scale to the analysis of monopoly.
- Explaining how a monopoly may adversely affect resource allocation.
- Drawing and explaining a diagram to show a monopoly restricting output and raising the price.
- Evaluating the costs and benefits of monopoly.

Examination questions

You should expect one multiple-choice question on monopolies and resource allocation. See MCQ 4 in Test 2 for an example. Because monopoly is an important cause of market failure, your knowledge and understanding of monopoly and market power are also likely to be tested by questions set on specification sections 10.5 ('Market failure') and 10.6 ('Government intervention in the market'). These areas of knowledge are covered in pp. 33–42 in this guide. DRQ 5 in the Question and Answer section shows how your knowledge of monopoly may be tested by a data–response question set on related key concepts, such as economies of scale and efficiency. A DRQ could also be set on a market dominated by large firms in which the data provide evidence of market power. From an examiner's point of view, data showing a previously natural monopoly, such as telecommunications being opened up to competition, would provide a fruitful scenario for a data–response question.

Common examination errors

Commonly made mistakes on monopolies and resource allocation include the following:
- Defining monopoly as a firm with 25% of the market.
- Asserting without any further justification that monopoly is always bad.
- Inability to distinguish between pure monopoly and monopoly power.
- Failure to identify monopoly as a cause of market failure.
- A lack of understanding of the significance of barriers to entry, which deter or prevent competition.
- Inability to apply key economic concepts such as efficiency to the analysis and evaluation of monopoly.
- Drifting into a long descriptive account of the causes of monopoly when the question requires analysis and evaluation of the *effects* of monopoly power.

Production and efficiency

These notes relate to AQA specification section 10.4 and prepare you to answer examination questions on the following:
- the meaning of production
- key concepts relating to production: specialisation and the division of labour; economies of scale; and efficiency

Essential information

Production is simply the process through which **inputs** are converted into **outputs**. The inputs into the production process are the four **factors of production** listed in Figure 7: **land**, **labour**, **capital** and the entrepreneurial input, often called **enterprise**.

The entrepreneur ultimately decides **what**, **where**, **how** and **how much to produce**, and also how much of the other factor services to employ. Economists assume that the entrepreneur (and the firm) has a **profit-maximising objective**. **Profit** is the difference between the **total sales revenue** earned from the sale of the goods or services produced by the firm, and the **total costs of production** incurred when paying the factors of production for their services. Profit is the entrepreneur's reward for decision-making and financial risk-taking.

Figure 7 A firm undertaking production

It is important for you to understand how the nature of production depends on the time period in which it takes place. In production theory, economists distinguish between three time periods: the **market period**, the **short run** and the **long run**. In the market period (which is also known as the **momentary period** and the **instantaneous period**), all the factors of production are fixed and cannot be varied. As a result, firms cannot increase production to meet an increase in demand, and supply is completely inelastic. In the short run, at least one factor of production (usually assumed to be capital or the firm's buildings, machinery, etc.) is fixed and cannot be varied. Supply may still be relatively inelastic. By contrast, in the long run, all the factors of production can be varied. The **scale** of the firm's **capacity** (which is fixed in the short run) can be increased. In the long run, supply is likely to be much more elastic.

The only way a firm can increase production in the short run is by employing more variable factors of production (e.g. labour). To start with, as more workers are employed, **labour productivity** (output per worker) may rise, as the workers benefit from **specialisation** and the **division of labour**, i.e. different workers specialising in different tasks. (In the economy as a whole, different firms and industries also specialise in producing different goods and services. This, of course, necessitates **trade** and **exchange**, which take place in the economy's markets.)

Eventually, however, when production approaches **full capacity**, the firm may decide to expand and increase the scale of its capacity. This is especially likely when **economies of scale** are possible. **Internal economies of scale** occur when growth in the size or scale of the firm itself causes average costs of production (or costs per unit of output) to fall. There are various types of internal economies of scale, such as technical and managerial economies. See DRQ 5 for an explanation of technical economies of scale. **External economies of scale** occur when a firm's average production costs fall as a result of the growth of the whole industry rather than

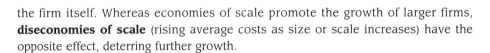

the firm itself. Whereas economies of scale promote the growth of larger firms, **diseconomies of scale** (rising average costs as size or scale increases) have the opposite effect, deterring further growth.

The level of output produced at the lowest average cost of production is known as the **productively efficient level of output**. When economies of scale are possible, expanding the size or scale of the firm can increase productive efficiency. The economy as a whole is said to be productively efficient when it is producing on its **production possibility boundary**. Take care not to confuse **productive efficiency** with **allocative efficiency**. When the economy is productively efficient, it is impossible to increase *production* of one good without reducing *production* of at least one other good. By contrast, allocative efficiency means that it is impossible to increase the *economic welfare* of one individual, consumer or household without reducing the *economic welfare* of at least one other. The allocation of goods and services between competing uses is then deemed to be optimal. The notes on 'Prices and resource allocation' (pp. 25–26) explain the **rationing** or **allocative function of prices**. Economists often argue that, when rationing scarce resources between competing uses, the price mechanism achieves an allocatively efficient outcome, providing markets perform well and are free of **market failure**. The notes on 'Public goods and externalities' (pp. 33–36) and 'Merit and demerit goods, and inequalities in the distributions of income and wealth' (pp. 36–39) explain that when the price mechanism fails to function properly, a misallocation of resources results. The outcome can be described as **allocatively inefficient**.

Examination skills

The skills most likely to be tested by multiple-choice and data–response questions on production and efficiency are as follows:
- Defining and explaining the meaning of production, specialisation, division of labour, economies of scale, productive efficiency and allocative efficiency.
- Discussing the reasons for the growth of a firm, or the advantages resulting from growth.
- Relating specialisation and the division of labour to the role of markets in the economy.
- Relating over-specialisation and diseconomies of scale to possible causes of market failure.
- Analysing monopoly in terms of economies of scale.

Examination questions

You should expect up to two multiple-choice questions on production and efficiency. See MCQ 12 in Test 1 for an example. DRQs 5 and 6 illustrate ways in which knowledge and understanding of the key concepts in this section of the specification may be tested in a data–response question. The scenario in DRQ 5 centres on economies of scale in the oil transportation industry, and then relates economies of scale to the emergence of monopolies. DRQ 6 illustrates one of the most important applications of specialisation and the division of labour, namely the international division of labour between countries (rather than different workers specialising in different tasks within a single firm). Market-based questions such as DRQs 1 and 2 could well ask for a discussion of whether the market functions efficiently. Practise the skill of assessing whether the market depicted in a data–response question is productively and allocatively efficient.

Common examination errors

Commonly made mistakes on production and efficiency include the following:
- Confusing short-run production and long-run production.
- Relating economies of scale to the short run rather than to the long run.
- Failure to appreciate how markets facilitate specialisation and the division of labour.
- Writing over-long descriptive accounts of types of economy of scale.
- Confusing internal and external economies of scale.
- Failure to understand and correctly apply the concepts of productive and allocative efficiency.

Public goods and externalities

These notes relate to AQA specification section 10.5 and prepare you to answer examination questions on the following:
- the failure of markets to provide public goods
- the tendency of a market to over-provide or under-provide a good when externalities are discharged in the course of the good's production or consumption

Essential information

A **public good**, such as the lighthouse shown in Figure 8, leads to a type of market failure known as a **missing market**: the market may simply fail to provide any quantity at all of a public good. To understand this, you should compare a public good with a private good. Most goods are **private goods**, possessing two important characteristics. The owners can exercise **private property rights**, preventing other people from using a good or consuming its benefits — unless they are prepared to pay a price for the good in the market. This property is called **excludability**. The second characteristic possessed by a private good is **diminishability**: when one person consumes the good, less of the benefits are available for other people. A **public good** exhibits the opposite characteristics of **non-excludability** and **non-diminishability** or non-rivalry. It is these that lead to market failure.

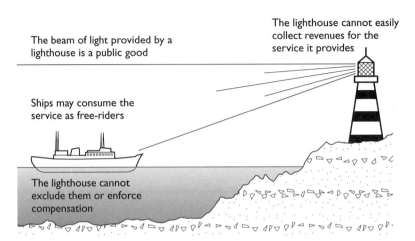

The beam of light provided by a lighthouse is a public good

The lighthouse cannot easily collect revenues for the service it provides

Ships may consume the service as free-riders

The lighthouse cannot exclude them or enforce compensation

Figure 8 A lighthouse as a public good

Suppose an entrepreneur builds the lighthouse shown in Figure 8, and then tries to charge each ship benefiting from the service provided, namely the beam of light. Providing ships pay up, the service can be provided commercially through the market. But the market is likely to fail because the **incentive function of prices** breaks down (see p. 26). Because it is impossible to exclude **free-riders** (ships that benefit without paying), it may be impossible to collect enough revenue to cover costs. If too many ships decide to 'free ride', profits cannot be made and the incentive to provide the service through the market disappears. The market thus fails to provide a service for which there is an obvious need; hence the case for alternative provision by the government in its **public spending programme**, or possibly by a charity.

You should distinguish between **pure** and **non-pure public goods**. National defence and police are examples of pure public goods — defined as public goods for which it is impossible to exclude 'free-riders'. However, most public goods (street lighting, roads, television and radio programmes and also lighthouses) are non-pure public goods. Methods can be devised for converting the goods into private goods by excluding 'free-riders' (for example, electronic pricing of road use). Non-pure public goods can be provided by markets, although the second property of non-diminishability or non-rivalry means there is a case for providing all public goods free in order to encourage as much consumption as possible. For public goods, the **allocatively efficient** level of consumption occurs when they are available free of charge.

An **externality** is a special type of public good or public 'bad' which is 'dumped' by those who produce it on other people (known as **third parties**) who receive or consume it, whether or not they choose to. The key feature of an externality is that there is no market in which it can be bought or sold — externalities are produced and received outside the market, providing another example of a 'missing market'.

As with the public goods, externalities provide examples of the 'free-rider' problem. The provider of an **external benefit** (or **positive externality**), such as a beautiful view, cannot charge a market price to any 'willing free-riders' who enjoy it, while conversely, the 'unwilling free-riders' who receive or consume **external costs** (or **negative externalities**), such as pollution and noise, cannot charge a price to the polluter for the 'bad' they reluctantly consume.

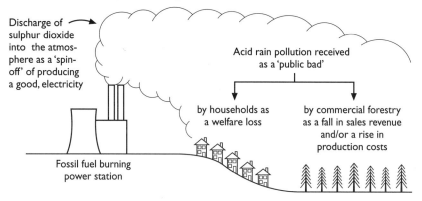

Figure 9 The discharge of a negative externality, atmospheric pollution, by a power station

Consider the power station illustrated in Figure 9, which discharges pollution into the atmosphere in the course of producing electricity. We can view a negative production externality such as pollution as being that part of the *true* or *real* costs of production which the power station evades by dumping the 'bad' on others. The price that the consumer pays for the good (electricity) reflects only the *money* costs of production, and not all the *real* costs, which include the external costs. In a market situation, the power station's output of electricity is thus under-priced. The incentive function of prices has once again broken down — under-pricing encourages too much consumption of electricity, and therefore over-production of both electricity and the spin-off, pollution.

Examination skills

The skills most likely to be tested by multiple-choice and data–response questions on public goods and externalities are as follows:
- Identifying examples of public goods and externalities.
- Explaining the reasons why market failure occurs in the case of public goods and externalities.
- Understanding the meaning of non-excludability and non-diminishability.
- Relating the market failure to the breakdown of the incentive function of prices.
- Explaining how over-consumption or under-consumption is allocatively inefficient.
- Assessing the case for government intervention to correct the market failure.

Examination questions

You should expect up to two multiple-choice questions on public goods and externalities. See MCQs 13 in Test 1 and 10 in Test 2 for examples. For space reasons, it has not been possible to include a data–response question in this guide on public goods or externalities, but important aspects of market failure which relate to some extent to public goods and externalities are covered by DRQs 3 and 4.

The data in a Unit 1 examination DRQ is more likely to be based on a public good, such as defence or television programmes, than on externalities. This is because many externalities, such as road congestion and pollution, are **environmental externalities**, the understanding of which will be tested in the Unit 3: Markets at Work examination rather than in the Unit 1 examination. The AQA advises: *'Providing candidates have developed a sound grasp of the economic principles specified in Modules 1 and 2, the information contained in the questions in the Unit 3 examination should be sufficient to allow candidates to answer the questions. While the Unit 3 questions draw on the subject content of both Modules 1 and 2, the questions are likely to be weighted slightly in favour of the microeconomic principles introduced in Module 1.'* Environmental externalities provide perhaps the most obvious case in point: the knowledge and principles learnt when studying externalities in Module 1 are most likely to be tested and assessed by an optional question on the environment in the Unit 3 examination.

Common examination errors

Commonly made mistakes on public goods and externalities include the following:
- Confusing a public good, such as defence, with a merit good, such as health care (see p. 37). (see p. 37)
- Wrongly defining a public good as a good provided by the government.
- Confusing a public good with a free good.
- Failing to explain *how* and *why* the market fails in the case of public goods and externalities.
- Not understanding that markets can and do provide public goods, providing methods are devised for excluding 'free-riders'.
- Naively arguing that government intervention always succeeds in correcting market failure.

Merit and demerit goods, and inequalities in the distributions of income and wealth

These notes relate to AQA specification section 10.5 and prepare you to answer examination questions on the following:
- under-consumption of merit goods
- over-consumption of demerit goods
- inequalities in the distributions of income and wealth

Essential information

A **merit good**, such as education or health care, is a good or service for which the **social benefits** of consumption enjoyed by the whole community exceed the **private benefits** received by the consumer. Consumption by an individual produces **positive externalities** that benefit the wider community.

As their name suggests, **demerit goods** are the opposite of merit goods. The **social costs** to the whole community which result from the consumption of a demerit good, such as tobacco or alcohol, exceed the **private costs** incurred by the consumer. This is because consumption by an individual produces **negative externalities** that harm the wider community. The private cost can be measured by the money cost of purchasing the good, together with any health damage suffered by the person consuming the good. But the social costs of consumption also include the cost of the negative externalities: for example, the costs of damage and injury inflicted on other people, resulting from tobacco smoke and road accidents caused by drunken drivers.

Whereas markets may fail to provide any quantity at all of a pure public good, such as defence, they can certainly provide education and health care, as the existence of private fee-paying schools and hospitals clearly demonstrates. But if schools and hospitals are available *only* through the market at prices unadjusted by subsidy, people (especially the poor) will choose to consume too little of their services. The resulting under-consumption of merit goods and over-consumption of demerit goods is **allocatively inefficient** (see p. 32). Government intervention to encourage the consumption of merit goods and discourage the consumption of demerit goods should improve allocative efficiency.

Merit goods and demerit goods can possess a further characteristic (besides the divergence between private and social costs and benefits) which leads to their under-consumption or over-consumption. Individuals consuming merit and demerit goods may not act in their own best interest because they consider only **short-term utility maximisation** rather than **long-term utility maximisation**. For the individual concerned, the **long-term private benefits** of consuming a merit good, such as education and health care, exceed the **short-term private benefits**. For example, in a market situation, many people under-purchase health care services such as regular dental checks, and end up suffering the consequences later in life. People are likely to choose too little of the merit good early in life, and later in life they may wish they had consumed more. This is an example of an **information problem**.

Similarly, with a demerit good such as tobacco, the **long-term private costs** of consumption can exceed the **short-term private costs**. A teenage boy or girl who develops a smoking habit may regret later in life the decision to start smoking, particularly if he or she eventually contracts a smoking-related disease. With both merit and demerit goods, many economists argue that an authority outside the individual, such as the state, is a better judge than individuals themselves of what is good for them. The state should thus encourage the consumption of merit goods and discourage the consumption of demerit goods for the individual's own interest, as well as for the wider social interest.

Merit goods	Merit or demerit goods?	Demerit goods
Education	Contraception	Tobacco
Health care (e.g. vaccination, dental care, AIDS testing)	Abortion	Alcohol
	Sterilisation	Heroin and other drugs
Crash helmets		Pornography
Car seat belts		Prostitution

Merit and demerit goods

The goods listed in the left-hand panel of the above table are generally regarded as merit goods, while those in the right-hand panel are considered to be demerit goods. However, for the 'goods' listed in the middle panel — for example, contraception — the position is less clear-cut. Because people have different values and ethics (often related to their religions), contraception is viewed by some people as a merit good, but by others as a demerit good. Whether a good is classified as a merit good or a demerit good, or indeed as neither, thus depends crucially on the value judgements of the person making the classification. This provides an important example of the distinction between **positive** and **normative** statements (see p. 13).

Likewise, economists have different views on whether inequalities in the distributions of income and wealth should be regarded as market failures. While there is general agreement that a completely unregulated market economy produces significant inequalities, some economists believe that government intervention to redistribute income and wealth destroys incentives that are vital for a market economy to function efficiently. In their view, such intervention leads to worse problems of **government failure** (see p. 41).

Examination skills

The skills most likely to be tested by multiple-choice or data–response questions on merit and demerit goods, and inequalities in the distributions of income and wealth are as follows:

- Explaining why a particular good is a merit good or a demerit good.
- Explaining why markets under-supply merit goods and over-supply demerit goods.
- Applying the concept of efficiency to the analysis of merit and demerit goods, and the concept of equity to the analysis of the distributions of income and wealth.
- Distinguishing between the distributions of income and wealth.
- Identifying appropriate government policies for correcting the market failures associated with merit and demerit goods, and the distributions of income and wealth (see pp. 39–42).
- Evaluating the extent to which these policies succeed in correcting the market failure.

Examination questions

You should expect up to two multiple-choice questions on merit and demerit goods, and inequalities in the distributions of income and wealth. See MCQs 11, 12 and 15 in Test 2 for examples. These market failures may feature in one of the two optional data–response questions. See DRQs 3 and 4 for examples. A merit good (health care) provides the scenario for DRQ 3, whereas the data in DRQ 4 centre on tobacco as a demerit good. Both questions test knowledge and understanding of how governments intervene in markets to try to correct market failures (see pp. 39–42) as well as the reasons why markets fail to provide the socially optimal quantity of merit and demerit goods (which is covered by these notes).

Common examination errors

Commonly made mistakes on merit and demerit goods, and inequalities in the distributions of income and wealth include the following:

- Wrongly classifying merit goods such as health care and education as public goods because they are often provided by the state in its public spending programme.
- Stating that merit goods are not private goods.
- Confusing a demerit good with an economic 'bad' — whereas a 'good' yields utility when consumed, a 'bad' such as pollution yields the opposite, namely **disutility**.
- Failing to understand that markets *can* produce merit and demerit goods, but they produce the 'wrong' (allocatively inefficient) quantity.
- Assuming that government intervention is always successful and corrects the market failure.
- Failing to recognise value judgements and the normative nature of these alleged market failures.
- Confusing wealth (a *stock* concept) with income (a *flow* concept).

Governments and markets

These notes relate to AQA specification section 10.6 and prepare you to answer examination questions on the following:

- the various ways in which governments intervene in markets to correct market failure and to improve economic welfare
- the situation known as government failure, which arises when government intervention in markets is unsuccessful or creates new problems

Essential information

This final topic in the specification for Module 1: Markets and Market Failure requires the application to the role of the government in markets of many terms and concepts you have studied earlier in this guide. Economists assume that governments intervene in markets to **maximise the social welfare** of the whole community, but like ordinary consumers and firms, governments face conflicts and **trade-offs** when trying to achieve their objectives (p.17). Indirect taxes and subsidies **shift supply curves**, while maximum and minimum prices cause **excess demand** and **excess supply** to emerge in markets (p.19). Elasticity (pp. 21–24) affects the impact of these and other forms of intervention. Taxes, subsidies and price controls also affect the **signalling, incentive** and **rationing functions of prices** (p. 26). Governments intervene in markets to correct various **market failures**: **monopoly** (pp. 27–30); **public goods** and **externalities** (pp. 33–36); and **merit goods**, **demerit goods** and **income** and **wealth inequalities** (pp. 36–39). The concept of **efficiency** (p. 32) should be applied to the analysis of all these attempts to correct market failure.

Figure 10 can be used to illustrate two different forms of government intervention in the market: the impact of **minimum price legislation** and the operation of a **buffer stock scheme** for an agricultural good such as rubber or coffee.

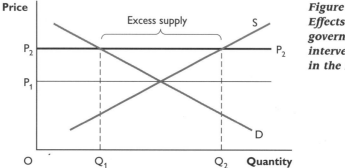

Figure 10
Effects of
government
intervention
in the market

Using Figure 10 to analyse the effect of price controls, price P_2 can be viewed as a minimum price or **floor price**, imposed by the government, below which it is illegal to trade. The **national minimum wage** in the **labour market** is an example. In effect, government intervention distorts the price mechanism and prevents the price falling to the equilibrium P_1. The market fails to clear and excess supply persists. (See MCQ 15 in Test 1 in the Question and Answer section of this guide for an example of a **maximum price control**, in this case a maximum rent in the housing market.)

To explain how Figure 10 can be used to illustrate a buffer stock scheme for a good such as coffee, we shall assume that a bumper harvest has shifted the supply curve rightwards to the position shown in the diagram. Because the market-clearing or equilibrium price P_1 is deemed too low, the government (or some other authority) sets an **intervention price** P_2 and begins **support buying** to take the excess supply off the market. Quantity $Q_2 - Q_1$ goes into a buffer stock, which may eventually be sold if a bad harvest shifts supply leftwards and raises the price to an unacceptably high level.

Examination questions

You should expect some aspect of government intervention in markets to figure in one or more of the wrong answers or the correct answer in a large number of the multiple-choice questions in the examination. For example, MCQs 1 and 15 in Test 1, and 9, 10, 11, 12, 13, 14 and 15 in Test 2 in the Question and Answer section of this guide all test understanding of at least one aspect of government intervention in markets. Government intervention in markets is also quite likely to feature in at least one part of a data–response question. See DRQs 3(d), 4(d) and 5(c) for examples. In all these questions, government intervention in markets appears in the last part of the question, which tests the 'higher-level' skill of evaluation. You must prepare to answer questions asking for a discussion of the case for and against intervening, or the advantages and disadvantages of a particular method of intervention in a market, such as imposing a tax or maximum price, operating a buffer stock scheme, or regulating the market.

Common examination errors

Commonly made mistakes on governments and markets include the following:
- Failure to relate intervention in markets to the government's objectives.
- Confusing the two main reasons why governments provide goods or services through state spending: because markets completely fail to provide public goods such as defence, and because they under-provide merit goods such as health care.
- Confusing objectives and methods of intervention.
- Describing methods of intervention when the question asks for evaluation of methods.
- Inability to use appropriate supply and demand diagrams to illustrate the effect of intervention.
- Assuming that government intervention is always successful and improves economic welfare.
- Failure to appreciate the many different ways in which governments can intervene, including state ownership and direct provision of goods and services.

Regulation and **taxation** are the main policy instruments that governmen achieve their objectives and to correct market failure. Regulation is used in a of ways: to deter monopoly abuse; to force people to consume merit goods seat belts); to restrict consumption of demerit goods; to control emission of externalities; and to promote positive externalities. By placing boundaries on markets can work, regulations constrain the market. In contrast, by alterin within the market, indirect taxes (and their opposite, subsidies) affect the si function of prices and the incentives that prices create for consumers an See MCQ 14 in Test 2 in the Question and Answer section of this guide for an (of a question testing analysis of the impact of an indirect tax on a market. taxes are commonly used by governments, alongside regulation, to disc consumption of demerit goods such as tobacco and, illustrating the **pollut(pay** principle, to punish firms and motorists for the externalities they dis **Subsidies** can be used to encourage consumption of merit goods (e.g. fre education and health care) and the production of positive externalities. **Per pollute** are another way of reducing negative externalities.

Examination candidates often assume, rather naively, that whenever gover intervene in the economy to correct market failure, they always succeed. This is not the case, and nowadays economists use the term **government failure** t(all the situations in which government intervention produces an unsatis outcome. Government failures range from the relatively trivial, when interver ineffective but where harm is restricted to the cost of resources used up and by the intervention, to cases when intervention produces new and much serious problems that did not exist before. For example, banning alcohol pr(the growth of illegal and criminalised 'underground' markets in which the socia of consumption may be far worse than in a legal market. As the specification 'governments may create rather than remove market distortions; inadequate inforr. conflicting objectives and administrative costs should be recognised as possible s of government failure'.

Examination skills

The skills most likely to be tested by multiple-choice or data–response questic governments and markets are as follows:
- Identifying the many different ways in which governments can intervene in ma
- Drawing supply and demand diagrams to illustrate the effect of government vention in markets.
- Relating government intervention to the correction of market failures.
- Appreciating that intervention may not be successful and that probler government failure may result.
- Evaluating the case for, or the effects of, intervention.
- Discussing the effects of reduced intervention (e.g. through deregulation), r than increased intervention.

Questions
&
Answers

Thisis section includes 36 examination-style questions designed to be a key learning, revision and exam preparation resource. There are 30 multiple-choice questions (MCQs) and six data–response questions (DRQs). The 30 MCQs are similar in layout, structure and style to two complete ECN1/1 papers of the Unit 1 examination. The questions can be used *en bloc* as part of trial or mock exams near the end of your course. Alternatively, as you study a topic in the Content Guidance section of this guide, you could refer selectively to particular MCQs in this section that assess aspects of the topic.

Likewise, you can use the DRQs in this section either as timed test questions in the lead-up to the examination or to reinforce your understanding of the specification subject matter, topic by topic, as you proceed through Content Guidance.

This section also includes:
- Correct answers for the MCQs.
- Examiner's comments on the MCQs, explaining particular features of each question, or possible causes of difficulty.
- A student's answer of grade A to C standard for each DRQ.
- Examiner's comments on each student's answer, explaining — where relevant — how the answer could be improved and a higher grade or mark achieved. These comments are denoted by the icon 🄔.

Note: it is important to understand the difference between two types of marks that the GCE examining boards award for candidates' work: 'raw marks' and uniform standardised marks (USMs).

Raw marks are the marks out of 25 awarded by the examiner who reads your script. After all the scripts have been marked, and basing their decisions only on raw marks, a grade-awarding panel decides where the grade boundaries should be set for each of the AS pass grades: A, B, C, D and E.

After all the grade boundaries have been set as raw marks, each candidate's raw mark for the Unit 1 paper is converted into a USM. Uniform standardised marks have the same grade boundaries — for all subjects and all unit exams. These are: grade A: 80%; grade B: 70%; grade C: 60%; grade D: 50%; grade E: 40%.

The marks awarded for candidates' answers for each of the DRQs in the following pages are raw marks and not USMs. A likely grade is indicated at the end of each candidate's answer, based on the qualities shown in each of the answer's three parts. It must be stressed that the actual raw mark at which a particular grade boundary is set varies from examination to examination, depending on factors such as whether the questions turned out to be relatively easy or relatively difficult, when compared to questions in previous examinations.

Multiple-choice questions: Test 1

1 Which of the following is a positive economic statement?
  A Education should be made available free for all children
  B Governments ought to intervene in the economy to correct market failures
  C A reduction in welfare benefits will increase the supply of labour
  D Imposing price controls is an unfair method of allocating resources

2

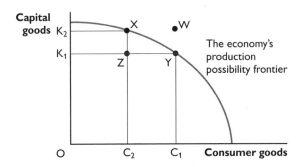

Which of the following statements relating to the production possibility frontier is NOT correct?
  A The opportunity cost of increasing the output of capital goods from K_1 to K_2 is sacrificed output of consumer goods of $C_1 - C_2$
  B Point W is more productively efficient than points X, Y and Z
  C Point Z is productively inefficient
  D Available economic resources are fully employed at points X and Y

3 A typical supply curve of a good shows:
  A the quantities of the good firms actually sell at different possible prices
  B the quantities of the good firms are prepared to supply at different possible prices
  C different possible equilibrium prices
  D quantity supplied varying inversely with price

4 The table below shows the quantity demanded of goods H and K at two different prices of good H.

Price of H	Quantity of H demanded	Quantity of K demanded
£5	50	100
£4	60	160

The cross elasticity of demand for good K with respect to the price of good H when the price of good H falls from £5 to £4 is:
  A −1.0
  C +1.0
  B −3.0
  D +3.0

multiple-choice questions

5 Average household disposable income rises from £1,500 to £1,800 per month, and as a result the demand of a typical household for groceries increases by 10%. From this information it can be concluded that for a typical household:

A groceries are an inferior good

B groceries are a normal good

C the demand for groceries is income elastic

D the income elasticity of demand for groceries is unity

6 When the demand curve for good A has a negative slope, a fall in the price of a substitute good B results in:

A an increase in the quantity demanded of good A

B a rightward shift in the demand curve for good A

C a leftward shift in the demand curve for good B

D a leftward shift in the demand curve for good A

7 Which of the following events might cause the demand curve for chicken meat to shift to the right?

A a fall in the price of chicken meat

B a fall in the price of turkey meat

C an outbreak of salmonella infection in chicken meat

D the publication of a health report urging people to eat white rather than red meats

8 Which of the following statements relating to price elasticity of supply in the following diagram is correct?

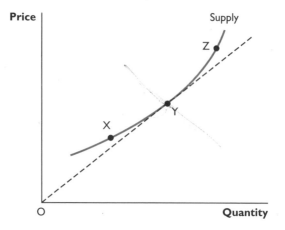

A Price elasticity of supply is inelastic at point X on the supply curve

B Price elasticity of supply is unit elastic at point Y on the supply curve

C Price elasticity of supply is elastic at point Z on the supply curve

D Price elasticity of supply has a constant value of unity at all points on the supply curve

9

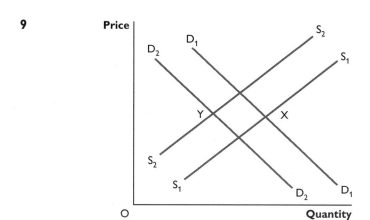

The diagram depicts the movement in the market for personal computers (PCs) from an initial equilibrium at point X to a subsequent equilibrium at point Y. Which of the following combination of events could explain the movement from X to Y?

A A rise in the price of a substitute good and a fall in the price of a complementary good

B The publication of a health report linking PC use with brain tumours and a fall in costs of production

C A fall in consumers' income and the removal of a government subsidy granted to PC manufacturers

D The removal of entry barriers to the PC industry and the use of television sets rather than PCs for accessing the Internet

10 Which of the following statements can be deduced from the table without the need for any additional information?

% of income spent on:	1947	1997
Food	34	14
Drink and tobacco	21	11
Rent and property tax	9	8
Fuel and light	7	4
Household goods	7	7
Clothing	10	6
Other goods	4	18
Services	8	32

Changing pattern of consumer expenditure in the UK

Source: *Family Expenditure Survey.*

A People bought less food in 1997 than in 1947

B People bought more drink and tobacco in 1947 than in 1997

C The price of clothing fell between 1947 and 1997

D Over the period, people spent an increasing proportion of their income on the output of the tertiary sector of the economy

11 Faced with falling prices and profits, a firm decides to leave one industry and move into another industry in which prices are rising, as are the profits of most firms already in the industry. Which of the following statements is correct?

multiple-choice questions

   A This illustrates the incentive function of prices
   B The demand curve shifts rightward in the market into which the firm is moving
   C There are no barriers to entry and exit separating the two industries
   D As a result of moving into the new industry, the firm's profits must increase

12 Economies of scale can result from all of the following EXCEPT one. Which is the EXCEPTION?
   A A factory employs two shifts of workers rather than one shift per day to make better use of fixed capacity
   B A bus company replaces smaller buses with larger buses
   C An increase in the size of a firm's capacity and plant
   D Increased firm size allowing the firm to employ specialist managers

13 To reduce acid rain pollution discharged by power stations, the USA has set up a market in tradable pollution permits. Which of the following statements about pollution permits is UNTRUE?
   A Pollution permits involve the 'polluter must pay' principle
   B Pollution permits involve some 'command and control' regulation
   C All affected power stations suffer financial penalty for polluting
   D The permits create incentives for power stations to reduce pollution

14 The diagram below shows world production of oil between 1999 and 2002.

World oil supply (millions of barrels per day)

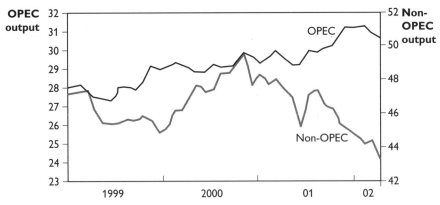

Source: *Financial Times*, 21 May 2002.

Which of the following can be concluded from the data?
   A OPEC oil output was greater than non-OPEC oil output throughout the period
   B Total oil production was at its greatest around the middle of the period
   C The price of non-OPEC oil rose and then fell
   D Oil-consuming countries increased their demand for OPEC oil because of its superior quality

15

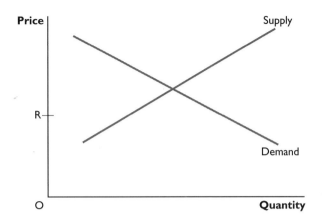

The diagram depicts the market for private rented housing, which is initially in equilibrium. The imposition by the government of a maximum rent of R must cause:

A the supply curve of rented housing to shift to the left

B the demand curve for private rented housing to shift to the right

C the price of owner-occupied housing to fall

D excess demand to occur in the market for private rented housing

Answers to multiple-choice questions: Test 1

1 C	**6** D	**11** A
2 B	**7** D	**12** A
3 B	**8** B	**13** C
4 B	**9** C	**14** B
5 B	**10** D	**15** D

Examiner's comments

Question 1

e The specification states: 'candidates should be able to distinguish between positive and normative statements'. This element of the specification is much easier to test in an objective test (or multiple-choice) question than in a data–response question, so it would be sensible to expect one question in each examination on the distinction between positive and normative statements. A positive statement is a statement of fact or definition (e.g. a metre contains 100 centimetres); or it is an assertion or prediction that may or may not be true, but which can be tested to see if it is true or false. The statement 'If the government abolishes the old age pension, many old people will die of malnutrition and cold' is positive. In principle, the assertion could be tested, although in practice, few if any people would wish to test it. By contrast, the other statements involve value judgements and are therefore normative.

Question 2

e A production possibility curve or frontier is one of the most useful diagrams in economics, and a favourite for multiple-choice questions. You must always be extra careful when, as in this question, you are asked to identify the odd one out, i.e. the *untrue* statement. It is so easy to read the question hurriedly and to choose the first *true* statement as the answer. In this question, A, C and D are true, and therefore *not* the answer. B, the only untrue statement, is the answer. While points X and Y are productively efficient, point W is not. W is located outside or beyond the production possibility frontier and is therefore unattainable.

Question 3

e A market supply curve shows *planned* or *intended* supply, i.e. the quantities of a good that firms *would like* to supply at different possible prices. Statement B is therefore the correct answer. Don't confuse this with statement A, which relates to *realised* or *fulfilled* supply, i.e. the quantities of the good that firms actually end up selling at different prices.

Question 4

e The sign (+ or −) of a cross elasticity of demand indicates whether two goods are substitutes (+ sign) or in joint demand (− sign), while the absolute size of the elasticity statistic indicates whether the demand relationship is elastic (> 1), inelastic (< 1) or unit elastic (= 1). In this case, a 20% *fall* in the price of good H induces a 60% increase in the demand for good K (indicating that H and K are complementary goods in elastic joint demand), so the cross elasticity of demand is −3.0. The correct answer is therefore B.

Question 5

From the information provided we can conclude, first, that groceries are a normal good (demand rises as income rises) and, second, that the demand for groceries is income *inelastic* (increases less than proportionately with income). Statements C and D are wrong because they relate respectively to elastic demand and unit elasticity of demand. An inferior good is one for which demand *falls* as income rises — the opposite of a normal good. Statement A is therefore wrong, leaving B as the correct answer.

Question 6

The part of the stem of the question relating to a demand curve having a negative slope is irrelevant. It has been included in the question simply to confuse and distract. The question is testing knowledge of factors that cause demand curves to shift. The correct answer is D. Because consumers demand more of the substitute good following the fall in its price, demand switches away from the good specified in the question. This causes the demand curve for the good to shift leftward — less of the good is demanded at all prices.

Question 7

This question tests the same area of economic theory as question 6: namely, causes of shifts in demand. In this case, the correct answer is D: the publication of the health report specified in the question would alter people's behaviour in favour of eating chicken and turkey (white meats) and away from red meats such as beef and lamb. The demand curve for chicken meat would therefore shift rightward.

Question 8

The elasticity varies from point to point moving along the non-linear (i.e. curved rather than a straight line) supply curve shown in the diagram. To decide whether supply is elastic, unit elastic or inelastic at any point such as X, Y or Z on the curve, you should draw a tangent to the curve at the relevant point and check the following:
- If the tangent intersects the price axis, supply is elastic.
- If the tangent intersects the origin, supply is unit elastic.
- If the tangent intersects the quantity axis, supply is inelastic.

Application of this rule shows that B is the correct answer: price elasticity of supply is unity at point Y on the supply curve.

Question 9

The diagram shows a leftward shift of both the demand and the supply curves. Only statement C includes *two* events that can account for the leftward shift of *both* curves. C is therefore the correct answer.

Question 10

Statement D is the correct answer, being the only one of the four statements that can be deduced from the table without the need for any additional information. The tertiary sector of the economy is made up of services — the last item in the table.

ultiple-choice questions

Question 11

The correct answer is A — the information in the question provides a neat example of the incentive function of prices. Statement B is wrong: in the long run, the *supply curve* rather than the *demand curve* shifts rightwards as new firms enter a market. Statement C is incorrect because, although the question implies that the firm can move easily between markets, we cannot be certain that there are *no* barriers deterring entry. The barriers may simply be very low. For a similar reason, statement D is wrong. The firm *hopes* to make bigger profits in the new market, but we cannot be certain that larger profits will materialise.

Question 12

Economies of scale can result from all the events specified in statements B, C and D, but not from the event specified in statement A. The correct answer is therefore A. Statement B relates to **volume economies of scale** (also known as **economies of increased dimension**), which are a type of **technical economy of scale**. Internal economies of scale result from an increase in a firm's production capacity, so statement C is true by definition. Statement D relates to **managerial economies of scale**. By contrast, statement A has nothing to do with economies of scale. Instead, it illustrates the economic short run.

Question 13

The system of pollution permits imposes a maximum pollution limit which has been reduced over a series of years. Since this involves 'command and control' regulation, statement B is correct. Power stations that reduce pollution by more than the limit requires can sell their 'spare' pollution permits to power stations that fail to comply, to enable the latter to continue to pollute within the law. This is an example of the 'polluter must pay' principle, so statement A is correct. Statement D is also correct, since the market creates incentives to reduce pollution to avoid the need to purchase 'spare' pollution permits. This leaves C as the only untrue statement and therefore the answer: under-complying power stations suffer financial penalty but the over-complying power stations that sell their 'spare' permits make a financial gain.

Question 14

The correct answer is B: by adding up the two data series, you can see that total oil production was at its highest level in late 2000. After this date, further growth in OPEC production was offset by a general fall in non-OPEC supply. Make sure you look carefully at the scales on both vertical axes. They tell you that non-OPEC production exceeded OPEC production throughout the period.

Question 15

For this question, statement D provides the correct answer, although C might be considered a *possible* answer. Whenever a maximum price control is imposed *below* the market-clearing equilibrium price (as is the case with rent OR), shortages and excess demand occur, leading to queues and waiting lists or other forms of quantity rationing. With regard to statement C, controls imposed on private rented housing *might* cause the price of owner-occupied housing to fall — for example, if the supply of houses for owner-occupation suddenly increased because landlords decided to sell houses they previously rented.

Multiple-choice questions: Test 2

1 The table gives the production possibility schedule for TV sets and radio sets. The opportunity cost of the third radio set in terms of TV sets is:

TV sets	Radio sets
17	0
16	1
14	2
12	3
9	4
6	5
3	6
0	7

A 2
B 3
C 4
D 12

2 The opportunity cost to society of building a fifth terminal at London Heathrow airport would be:

A the other goods or services which could be produced if the terminal were not built
B the second terminal at Gatwick airport, London's second airport
C the fact that the land on which the terminal is built cannot be used as farmland
D the lost opportunity to employ the building workers on other civil engineering schemes

3 The diagram below shows the number of package holidays sold through travel agents in the UK in millions, between 1991 and 1996.

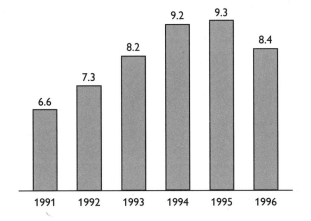

Which of the following can be concluded from the data?

A From 1991 to 1995 package holidays were a normal good but then they became an inferior good
B The demand curve for holidays shifted leftward in 1996
C The price of package holidays increased over most of the period shown by the data
D The demand for other types of holiday may have increased in 1996

multiple-choice questions

4 Which of the following is least likely to increase the competitiveness of a market?
  A An increase in the number of buyers and sellers in the market
  B A lowering of entry barriers separating markets
  C A decrease in the use of informative advertising in the market
  D Employers making greater use of the Internet to advertise job vacancies

5 The graph below shows average UK house prices for the period 1995–2001

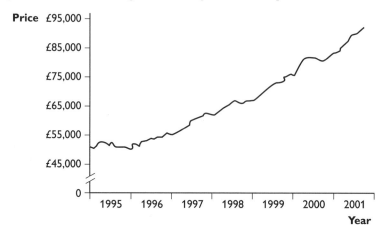

Source: *Daily Telegraph*, 29 December 2001.

Which of the following would best explain the rising trend in average house prices shown in the data?
  A A sustained growth in household income combined with a shortage of land for house building
  B An increase in mortgage interest rates
  C An increase in average household size
  D Owner-occupiers regarding a house as somewhere to live rather than as an investment

6 The table below shows estimates of elasticities of demand for apples and oranges taken from the National Food Survey.

	Elasticity with respect to:		
	price of apples	price of oranges	income
Apples	−0.29	−0.07	+0.32
Oranges	−0.16	−1.33	+0.14

Which of the following can be concluded from the data?
  A Apples and oranges are in joint demand
  B Apples but not oranges are inferior goods
  C The demand for apples is both price inelastic and income inelastic
  D The demand for oranges is both price elastic and income elastic

7

	Prices (annual % change)			
	1998	1999	2000	2001
Cocoa	−10.3	−32.0	−32.1	+13.1
Coffee	−28.5	−23.2	−2.2	−19.1
Tea	−1.0	−12.8	+4.1	+6.0

	Stocks (annual % change)			
	1998	1999	2000	2001
Cocoa	−10.3	−4.1	+9.4	0.0
Coffee	−7.8	+5.2	+10.0	+25.6
Tea	+8.8	−8.9	+8.3	+2.6

Which of the following conclusions can be inferred from the above tables?

A Intervention buying and selling to support the price of cocoa was suspended in 2001
B The price of coffee fell relative to the price of tea over the period 1998 to 2001
C The accumulation of a buffer stock completely failed to stabilise the price of coffee
D On average, tea was more expensive than coffee over the period 1998 to 2001

8 Whenever demand for a good is price elastic, an increase in price will:
A increase monopoly power
B increase consumer expenditure on the good
C increase consumer expenditure on a good in joint demand
D decrease total consumer expenditure on the good

9

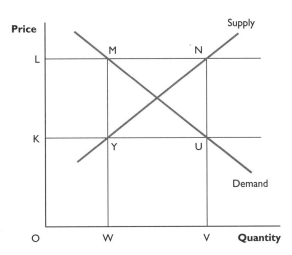

In the market illustrated in the diagram, the government imposes a minimum legal price of OL and guarantees to buy any excess supply at this price. Total government expenditure on the good will be shown by the area:

A WMNV
B OLMW
C YMNU
D OLNV

multiple-choice questions

10 Which of the following statements about public goods is correct?

A Public goods are defined as those goods provided by the state

B Public goods are examples of 'free goods'

C Public goods are characterised by the 'free rider' problem

D The problem of scarcity does not affect the provision of public goods

11 Whenever a government provides health care services free of charge:

A economic welfare is maximised

B government expenditure on the provision of public goods increases

C the incentive to provide private health care through the market completely disappears

D provision of a merit good by the state is taking place

12 Which of the following is an example of government regulation of the economy?

A The government selling a state-owned industry such as Air Traffic Control to private ownership

B The government announcing the abolition of rules that restrict the number of commercial radio stations allowed by law to operate

C The government encouraging the General Medical Council to discipline professionally negligent doctors

D A legal requirement enforced by local authorities that seat belts be fitted in all coaches and mini-buses

13 When the government intervenes in the market economy to correct a 'market failure':

A the problem of 'government failure' may result

B economic welfare always increases

C in all cases the market mechanism ceases to function

D the intervention has no opportunity cost

14

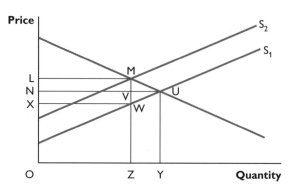

In the diagram, an indirect tax has been levied on a good, causing the supply curve to shift upward from S_1 to S_2. The amount of tax borne by the producers is equal to the area:

A XLMW

C XNUW

B NLMV

D XNVW

15 Which of the following statements about a highly unequal distribution of income is untrue?

A It may result from the inequitable functioning of markets

B It may result from an unsatisfactory allocation of resources

C It can be corrected by imposing indirect taxes on goods with a negative income elasticity of demand

D It is likely to occur in an economy subject to minimum government intervention

Answers to multiple-choice questions: Test 2

1	A	**6**	C	**11**	D
2	A	**7**	B	**12**	D
3	D	**8**	D	**13**	A
4	C	**9**	A	**14**	D
5	A	**10**	C	**15**	C

Examiner's comments

Question 1

e When scarce resources are used to produce radio sets, the same resources cannot be employed to produce television sets. If a firm redeploys capital and labour away from television set production in order to produce more radios, the opportunity cost of the extra radios is measured by the television sets that can no longer be produced. In this question, two television sets are sacrificed when the third radio set is produced, so A is the correct answer.

Question 2

e While statements C and D each specify an element in the opportunity cost of building a fifth terminal at London's Heathrow airport, statement A provides a more inclusive specification of the opportunity cost and is therefore the correct answer. Statement B is meaningless.

Question 3

e Only the last statement can be concluded from the data, so D is the answer. If package holidays fall in number, it is probable that holiday-makers have switched to substitutes, namely other forms of holiday. Statement A is hardly likely to be correct, as goods do not suddenly change from being normal goods (for which demand rises with income) to becoming inferior goods (for which demand falls as income rises). Statement B would be correct if it referred solely to package holidays, but because it refers to *all* categories of holiday it is incorrect. Statement C is *possibly* correct, but this cannot be concluded from the data.

Question 4

e The words 'least likely' in the stem of a question can throw a candidate who reads the question too hurriedly. However, this should not be a problem with this question (unless the words are misread as 'most likely') because all the events specified in statements A, B and D clearly tend to increase the competitiveness of a market. This leaves C as the correct answer. A decrease in the use of informative advertising would reduce rather than increase market competitiveness. (Arguably, however, much advertising that claims to be informative contains the opposite: namely, misleading and inaccurate claims about a product's supposed virtues. Such advertising, based on providing misinformation rather than information, is anti-competitive rather than competitive.)

Question 5

e Statement A provides the correct answer. Both events in the statement put upward pressure on house prices. B is obviously wrong since higher mortgage interest rates reduce demand for housing. C is also wrong. Although an increase in average household size would increase demand for larger houses, the demand for smaller houses (which form most of the UK housing stock) would fall. In any case, average household size has been falling in the UK with more single person households, and smaller households add to the upward pressure in house prices. D is wrong because, compared with countries like Germany, UK residents buy houses as an investment, as wealth assets. As the recent 'buy-to-let' fashion has shown, by adding to demand, this also puts upward pressure on house prices.

Question 6

e The cross elasticity of demand for apples with respect to the price of oranges is –0.07 while that for oranges with respect to the price of apples is –0.16. Both cross elasticities are negative, so apples and oranges are slight substitutes, rather than in joint demand. A is therefore wrong. B is also wrong as both goods have positive income elasticities of demand (+0.32 and +0.14 respectively) and are therefore normal goods. C is the correct answer: the price and income elasticity of demand for apples are both less than 1 (ignoring the minus sign for the price elasticity). The first part of statement D is correct, demand for oranges being price elastic, but the second part is wrong: demand for oranges is income inelastic.

Question 7

e Statement B provides the correct answer, being the only statement that can be inferred or deduced from the information in the two tables. The information in the top part of the table tells us that over the whole period 1998–2001 the prices of both coffee and tea fell. However, the price of coffee fell by a much larger cumulative percentage — partly because the rise in the price of tea in 2000 and 2001 partially offset the earlier fall in the price of tea. Thus we can conclude that the price of coffee fell *relative* to the price of tea over the 4 years. None of the other three statements can be inferred from the data, although this is not to say that statements A and D are wrong. With regard to statement C, buffer stock intervention might well have *partially* stabilised the price of coffee, so we cannot conclude that such intervention — if it occurred — was *completely* unsuccessful.

Question 8

e This question is testing knowledge of an important rule relating to elasticity, in this case price elasticity of demand. The rule is if, following an increase in price, consumers' total expenditure (or firms' total revenue):
- falls, then demand is elastic
- increases, then demand is inelastic
- remains the same, then demand is unit elastic

Applying this rule, it is clear that D is the correct answer.

multiple-choice questions

Question 9

The minimum legal price imposed by the government, OL, is above the equilibrium price: namely, the price located at the intersection of the supply and demand curves. Because the minimum legal price is set *above* the equilibrium price, excess supply occurs in the market. Since the government guarantees to take the excess supply off the market, its total expenditure (amount bought, multiplied by the price paid) is shown by the area WMNV. The correct answer is therefore A.

Question 10

A public good such as national defence or street lighting possesses the characteristic of non-excludability which creates the 'free rider' problem. Statement C is the answer. If a public good is provided for one person, it is provided for all in the sense that it is impossible to exclude other people from receiving the good's benefits. As a result, many people may be tempted to 'free ride' (a 'free rider' being a person who benefits without paying), which in turn causes the incentive function of prices to break down. The ability to charge a price provides the incentive for entrepreneurs to provide goods through markets. But when people can benefit without paying, the incentive function of prices breaks down because private entrepreneurs cannot sell the goods profitably. In extreme cases, complete market failure results, i.e. the market collapses completely, resulting in a 'missing market'.

Question 11

Most economists argue that health care is an example of a merit good, so statement D is the correct answer. By contrast with a public good, for which markets may fail to provide any quantity at all (resulting in 'missing' markets), markets can and do provide merit goods. However, if left solely to the market, merit goods such as health care end up being under-provided. Prices deter consumption, resulting in a level of production and consumption that is below the socially optimal level. As a result, economic welfare is not maximised. However, it does not follow that statement A is correct. The government may *try* to maximise economic welfare by providing a merit good free of charge, but this does not mean it always succeeds.

Question 12

This question is testing knowledge of methods of government intervention in the market economy. Statement A is an example of *privatisation* rather than *regulation*, so it is not the answer. Statement B is also wrong, being an example of *deregulation* or the abolition of previously imposed rules or regulations. Statement C does provide an example of regulation, *self-regulation* by the members of a profession, albeit with government encouragement, rather than external regulation of the profession by the government. This leaves statement D as the answer. According to the statement, the regulation has been imposed by central government and enforced by local government.

Question 13

The correct answer is A: government intervention in the market economy to correct market failure may be unsuccessful and create new problems that provide examples of 'government failure'.

Question 14

Expenditure taxes or indirect taxes imposed on firms are one of the factors that cause supply curves to shift upwards or leftwards. From firms' point of view, the tax is equivalent to a rise in the costs of production. Just as with a cost increase, firms will try to pass the tax on to consumers by raising the price of the good. However, firms' ability to *shift the incidence* of the tax by raising the price is limited by the elasticity of the demand curve. Except in the special case when demand is completely inelastic, demand falls as the price is raised. In the example depicted in the question, the firms can increase the price to OL, at which quantity OZ is bought and sold, but no higher. The total tax paid to the government is shown by the rectangle XLMW. This divides into two smaller rectangles, NLMV and XNVW, which lie respectively above and below ON, which was the equilibrium price *before* the tax was imposed. NLMV is the part of the tax passed on to consumers as a price rise (the shifted incidence of the tax), whereas XNVW must be borne by the producers (the unshifted incidence of the tax). XNVW is the correct answer: statement D.

Question 15

Statements A, B and D are all true, so do not provide the correct answer. This leaves statement C as the answer. Because **indirect taxes** (which are mostly **expenditure taxes**) raise the prices of goods, *real incomes* are reduced for all people who buy the goods. Of course, if indirect taxes were imposed on luxuries bought only or mainly by the rich, the distribution of real income would become more equal. But since statement C specifies that the indirect taxes are imposed on goods with a negative income elasticity of demand, this is not the case. Such goods are **inferior goods** bought primarily by the poor.

d ata–response question 1

Data–response questions

Question 1 The pulp market

Total for this question: 25 marks

Study **Extracts A**, **B** and **C**, and then answer **all** parts of the question which follow.

Extract A: Changes in Nordic pulp prices, 1995–2001

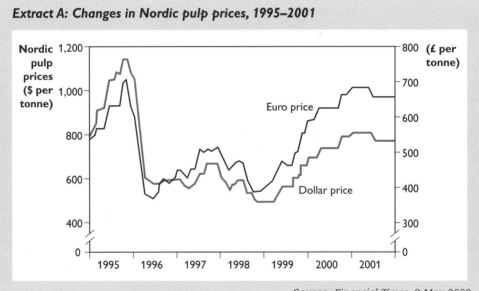

Source: *Financial Times*, 9 May 2000.

Extract B: Pulp enjoys rare balance between supply and demand

Strong demand, low levels of producer stocks and stable levels of paper-making capacity have created an environment that seems to favour a sustained upward movement in the prices of forest industry products.

After suffering from the effect of the Asian crisis in 1998, the price of pulp — the raw material used to make paper — slumped to a low point of around $460 a tonne early in 1999, before rising to $630 in February 2000. Stocks of raw material held by producers in North America and Scandinavia (the Nordic area) are the lowest for a February since 1995. In the run-up to January 2000, there was concern that prices were being driven up by unusually large consumption prompted by fears that around the millennium, supplies would be disrupted by the Year 2000 computer bug problem.

Adapted from *Financial Times*, 17 February 2000.

> ### Extract C: The need for price stability
>
> So far pulp manufacturers have been able to pass on most of the increases in their costs to end-users, but several are beginning to feel the squeeze on their profit margins. A leading pulp manufacturing company has recently called for price stability. In the past, rapid rises in pulp prices have prompted customers to build up stocks, which can then be used to force down the cost of the raw material. Pulp prices have then halved over the next 6 months. In the long run, neither the producers nor the users of paper pulp benefit from such price volatility.
>
> Adapted from *Financial Times*, 9 May 2000.

(a) **Extract A shows changes in the price of pulp over the period 1995 to 2001, measured in euros and US dollars. Compare the changes in the dollar price of pulp with the changes in the euro price.** (4 marks)

(b) **With the help of a supply and demand diagram, explain why, according to Extract B, the price of pulp rose in 1999 and 2000.** (6 marks)

(c) **Discuss how fluctuations in the price of pulp, such as those shown in the data, may affect other markets in the economy.** (15 marks)

■ ■ ■

Candidate's answer

(a) During the course of 1995, there was a strong rise in both the dollar and the euro prices of Nordic wood pulp, with the dollar price rising higher. The dollar and the euro price both fell sharply at the beginning of 1996. The euro price then recovered more quickly than the dollar price, overtaking it near the end of 1996. In the period 1997–98, the two prices followed each other closely, with the euro price slightly higher. During 1999, both prices rose steadily, with the euro price rising rather faster than the dollar price. Both prices flattened off during 2000 and 2001, with a slight fall at the end of the period. **3/4 marks**

📕 More often than not, part (a) of a data question will ask you either to describe the main features or changes in a graph or table, or to compare two data series. This is an example of the second type of question: the question asks for a comparison of changes in the price of Nordic pulp measured in two currencies, the US dollar and the euro. With this type of question, it is important not to stray beyond the relatively simple task you are asked to do.

The candidate sticks to answering the question and earns 3 of the available 4 marks, but fails to earn the extra mark because she describes the changes in too generalised a way, making insufficient use of the data. To earn full marks, it would be necessary to identify particular prices at key points in the data series. Alternatively, key percentage changes might be quoted (e.g. both prices falling by around 50% in the first half of 1996).

data–response question 1

(b) In 1999 and through 2000, the price of pulp increased. There were both supply and demand side factors to blame. Firstly, the low level of stocks of raw materials mentioned in Extract A meant that in the short run, the supply of pulp would be relatively inelastic. Pulp manufacturers could not increase supply to meet a sudden increase in demand. These supply conditions are illustrated by the nearly vertical inelastic supply curve S_1 on the diagram below:

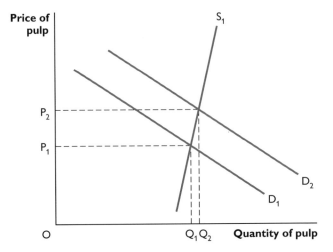

However, the increase in price is mainly explained by a rightward shift of demand — from D_1 to D_2 in the diagram. The main reason stated in Extract A for the increase in demand is increased demand for paper (being the raw material for paper, the demand for pulp is a derived demand), presumably because users of paper such as book publishers decided to print before the millennium to avoid disruption to production which they feared might be caused by the 'millennium bug'. Extract A also mentions that the Asian crisis of 1998 caused the price of pulp to fall in 1998 and early 1999. The recovery of demand for paper as the Asian economies recovered was probably a further factor causing the demand curve for pulp to shift from D_1 to D_2, and the price to rise from P_1 to P_2. **6/6 marks**

> *e* The candidate writes a perfect answer to this question, drawing an accurate supply and demand diagram, which she explains clearly in the text of her answer. Consequently, she earns all 6 marks.

(c) Fluctuations in the price of pulp will affect two other sets of markets: markets for forestry products and markets for pulp products such as paper making and book and newspaper publishing. Pulp making is the intermediary between these markets.

Pulp manufacturers buy timber from the forestry product industry. Timber is the raw material which is processed by the pulp companies. A sudden rise in the price of pulp (such as the rises which occurred in 1995 and 1999) should increase the profits of the timber producers, assuming that the rise in the price of pulp results from increased demand, which in turn increases the demand for the raw material, timber. Conversely a fall in the price of pulp, such as that resulting from a fall in demand for pulp products in Asia in 1998, will also result in a fall in demand for timber, probably reducing the profits of timber producers. Since most timber producers are located in Canada and Scandinavia rather than the UK, these effects will fall more heavily on overseas economies rather than the UK. However, as most timber used in the UK is imported, a rise in timber prices may adversely affect the UK's balance of payments, whereas a price fall would reduce the value of timber imports.

There are, of course, other uses for timber besides pulp making. A significant rise or fall in the price of pulp might cause forest product firms to divert output between alternative uses such as furniture making and pulp manufacturing, depending on which offered the best price for timber. But because higher quality timber is used for furniture rather than for pulp making, this factor is not likely to be significant.

A significant rise in the price of pulp would increase the costs of production of newspapers and books. According to the incentive function of prices, this would create an incentive for publishers to economise on the use of pulp. One way of doing this would be to make greater use of recycled paper rather than pulp produced from newly-cut timber. Unless newspaper and book publishers can cut costs elsewhere, however, for example by using thinner paper or fewer pages in newspapers, their profits will fall and/or they will have to put up prices. Depending on price elasticity and cross elasticity of demand, higher prices would then cause consumers to switch to alternative products such as electronic publications on the Internet.

A significant fall in the price of pulp would induce effects in other markets which are the opposite of those I have just discussed. **15/15 marks**

e This question provides a good example of the type of question you should expect for part (c) of a Unit 1: Markets and Market Failure data–response question. The question asks you to consider how events in the data — in this case, changes in the price of pulp — might affect other parts of the economy about which no information is given in the extracts. You should regard this as a possible 'house style' for the last part of a Unit 1 data question.

Also, as will sometimes be the case in part (c), the key instruction word is 'discuss'. For this question, the instruction to discuss means that you should indicate in your answer whether you think the effects you are noting in other markets, induced by changes in the price of pulp, are significant or not, and then give some justification of your reasoning.

While the candidate's answer is not perfect, she has done more than enough to earn full marks by discussing possible effects of changes in the price of pulp both in markets for inputs used in the pulp market and in markets for the industry's output. The candidate could improve her answer by developing the points she makes about price and cross elasticity of demand. Also, the effects in other markets might be

rather different if the causes of changes in the price of pulp lay in changes in the price of timber (the input into pulp making) rather than in increased demand for pulp exercised by newspapers etc. The candidate might have discussed this issue, possibly leaving out the point about the balance of payments. This point, while true, does not concern markets, so it earns no marks.

Scored 24/25   96% = high grade A

Question 2 The toy and watch markets

Total for this question: 25 marks

Study **Extracts A**, **B** and **C**, and then answer **all** parts of the question which follow.

Extract A: The market for Spice Girl dolls in December 1997

Extract B: What they really, really want for Christmas — and won't get

Spice Girl dolls will be on sale this Christmas. But only between 75,000 and 100,000 will make it to the shops — and not until the end of the second week in December.

Waiting in the queue for hours, just to see the last Posh or Scary disappear in front of your eyes, will be enough to send normally mild-mannered people into 'toy rage'. But one person's frustration is another's commercial opportunity. The shortage of the prized toys will lead to a black market. 'Toy touts' and their agents are queuing up to get the toys and then sell at a profit. The Spice Dolls are due to be retailed at just £20 each, but could be resold for four times that amount.

The Spice Girls negotiated for 2 months with the manufacturers about product specification. Frequent disagreements held up supply. All the members of the group were keen to check every detail. A prototype, which had Posh Spice smiling, had to be scrapped because her speciality is pouting. The company which markets the dolls intends to ration out the limited supply of dolls equitably among retail outlets. The fact that the dolls are made in China is expected to add to the supply problems.

Adapted from Independent, 17 October 1997.

data–response question 2

> **Extract C: The black market in Swatch watches**
>
> Anywhere in the world where young Italians gather, you will find a black market in Swatch watches. Buy one of the most sought-after models, the Chrono, the Scuba or the Automatic, for around £45, and you will have no trouble selling it again for twice as much. The people at Swatch know all about this black market; indeed some observers think they encourage it.
>
> Each Swatch is sold at a fixed price throughout the world. The price is deliberately low and supply is restricted. Only a few of each popular model will go to any particular shop at a time. This is puzzling: queues and black markets are usually signs of under-pricing. Swatch, it seems, could make more money either by raising its prices or by expanding supply.
>
> Adapted from *The Economist*, 8 February 1992.

(a) Explain the meaning of the terms 'equilibrium price' and 'excess demand' as used in Figure 1. (4 marks)

(b) Explain the causes of the black markets described in Extracts B and C. (6 marks)

(c) Discuss whether producers and consumers benefit from black markets such as those described in Extracts B and C. (15 marks)

■ ■ ■

Candidate's answer

(a) The equilibrium price is the one price in Extract A, which shows the market for Spice Girl dolls, where supply equals demand. At this point (i.e. where the supply and demand curves cross) the planned demand of buyers equals the planned supply of sellers in the market. If this is the market price, nobody is unhappy.

Excess demand occurs because there is a greater demand for Spice Girl dolls than there is supply. The excess demand shows the shortage of dolls in the market. **3/4 marks**

> 🖉 The candidate's answer shows a good understanding of both equilibrium price and excess demand, but earns 3 rather than all 4 of the available marks. He explains that, at the equilibrium price, *planned* demand equals *planned* supply. His statement that 'nobody is unhappy', while slightly clumsy, shows that he appreciates that when the market is in equilibrium, both consumers and producers can fulfil their market plans, respectively buying and selling all they want at the equilibrium price (£80 in Extract A).
>
> However, while the candidate clearly understands the meaning of excess demand, he drops a mark because he does not explain that excess demand occurs when the price is set below the equilibrium or market-clearing price. A perfect answer would explain how, in Extract A, at the £20 price set by the distributors, approximately

180,000 Spice Girl dolls are demanded, with only 75,000 being supplied, with the resulting excess demand being approximately 105,000.

(b) Black markets or secondary markets occur in markets in which demand for a good outstrips the producers' willingness or ability to supply that good. The producers' inability to supply enough is reflected in Extract B, which states that not enough dolls could be produced to satisfy demand. By contrast, Extract C demonstrates the lack of willingness by the manufacturer to supply Swatch watches to meet demand. The price and supply of both products were fixed by the producers below the equilibrium level, which encouraged the emergence of a black market as a mechanism for eliminating the excess demand occurring at the price set by the producers. **4/6 marks**

e The candidate's answer is short and to the point, earning 4 of the available 6 marks. He recognises that, while both black markets result from the producers under-pricing their goods, the black markets in Spice Girl dolls and Swatch watches have different underlying causes. The black market in Spice Girl dolls resulted from the producer's inability to increase supply to meet demand. By contrast, the black market in Swatch watches was deliberately created by the manufacturer, probably as a marketing ploy to create an exclusive brand image.

To earn all 6 marks, the candidate needs to develop his explanations more fully, using economic terms such as 'elasticity' and 'shifts of demand'.

(c) Producers would seem to benefit little from a black market for their products, especially in the relative short term when the good is under-supplied in relation to demand. Underpricing results in lost revenue and profit. However, a black market may be attractive for a producer as it helps to create brand loyalty and to increase the inelasticity of demand. The producers can also be confident that they will sell all the goods they produce. The high price for the good on the black market may also increase demand for the product on the legal market.

There are also advantages and disadvantages of a black market for consumers. The very notion of a black market suggests there is disequilibrium in the market, with many consumers not being able to obtain the good. The presence of 'touts' in the market will force consumers who do want the good to pay a higher price in the black market. Touts rather than customers benefit. However, a black market could be viewed as a fair way of distributing a limited supply of a good, as the people who gain the most utility from the good will be in the best position to obtain it. But it will be more difficult to obtain the good due to the presence of 'touts'. **9/15 marks**

e The candidate structures his answer quite well, discussing the disadvantages and advantages first for producers, and then for consumers. However, there are two weaknesses in this answer which reduce the total mark awarded to 9, which is at the top of the Level 3 mark range of 7–9 marks. One of the weaknesses is a failure to come to any sort of overall conclusion required by the instruction: 'discuss'. For this question, a discussion requires consideration of advantages and disadvantages

(both for producers and for consumers), followed by a conclusion that assesses the relative merits of the points made and/or whether the advantages exceed the disadvantages or vice versa.

The second weakness is a failure to develop sufficiently the points that the candidate does make with regard to the disadvantages and advantages of black markets. The points made tend to be assertions rather than properly reasoned explanations of advantage or disadvantage. For example, the candidate picks up the point about the manufacturers of Swatch encouraging the development of a black market, but restricts his answer to the assertion, without explanation, that a black market 'helps to create brand loyalty and to increase the inelasticity of demand'.

When discussing the advantages of black markets for consumers, the candidate might have explained that the black market or secondary market is a response to market failure in the primary market. A black market performs a useful economic function, enabling the 'lucky' customers who bought the good on the primary market but who are prepared to resell at a price higher than the price set in the primary market, to trade with the 'unlucky' customers who are prepared to pay a higher price. However, black markets are characterised by poor market information, with the middlemen or 'touts' who function as market-makers often being the main beneficiaries. A black market is an example of what economists call a 'second-best' solution; the 'first-best' or more desirable outcome would be an efficient primary market with goods being bought and sold at the equilibrium price — in which case there would be no need for a black market.

Scored 16/25   64% = grade B/C boundary

Question 3 Health care

Total for this question: 25 marks

Study **Extracts A**, **B** and **C**, and then answer **all** parts of the question which follow.

Extract A: Queues and the National Health Service

When health care is provided free, a queue rather than the price mechanism rations scarce resources between competing uses. A queue is a good example of a non-price rationing mechanism. Even if the money price of a good is zero, the *opportunity cost* of the time spent queuing will act as a non-monetary price: the longer the queue, the higher is the 'price', and the lower is the incentive to join the queue.

Since medical treatment within the NHS is normally free in monetary terms for the consumer, one might think of a waiting list as a rationing device that reduces effective demand for health services to the level of the available supply. But waiting lists in the NHS are also frequently used as evidence for a need to increase the resources devoted to the NHS. The perception of waiting lists as a symptom of excess demand has typically led to a supply response which involves an increase in resources.

Adapted from the 'Economics of NHS waiting lists' in *Economic Review*, May 1988.

Extract B: Patient treatment frontier

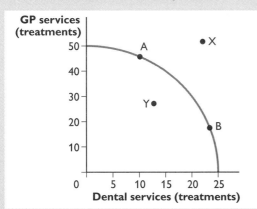

Suppose a health authority has to provide just two services to the community: general practitioner (GP) services and dental services. A patient treatment frontier, which is an example of a production possibility frontier, shows some of the trade-offs facing the health authority.

Extract C: Health rationing

Economics is all about rationing. In everyday markets, price adjustments reconcile demand and supply, and commodities are rationed on the basis of willingness to pay. Individuals with both the desire and the purchasing power obtain the goods, and those without either one or the other, or both, do not.

data-response question 3

Private health care in the UK, such as non-prescription pills and potions available in the local pharmacy, works in the same fashion. The NHS, however, has always functioned differently. With care being funded from taxation and delivered free to all, rationing by price could never be applied. In the past, direct means of rationing have been employed, principally delay and denial.

Rationing-by-quantity has been fundamental to the NHS since its creation in 1948 although, until the 1980s, the public was largely unaware of it. At times of excess demand for a given service, potential customers have been obliged to queue, in the form of having to join a waiting list for a given treatment. Moreover, as medical technologies have developed in other countries, the NHS has often been slow to make the new technologies available, limiting potential demand by failure to supply.

Adapted from 'UK health care: reorganisation and rationing', in *New Developments in Economics*, Vol. 16, 2000.

(a) Define the concept of opportunity cost which is mentioned in Extract A, and explain how the patient treatment frontier in Extract B illustrates opportunity cost within the health service. (4 marks)

(b) Explain how the data illustrate the economic problem of scarcity and identify the various methods mentioned in the data of resolving the problem of excess demand. (6 marks)

(c) Making use of the data and your economic knowledge, discuss the case for using queues and waiting lists as the main method of rationing demand within the NHS. (15 marks)

■ ■ ■

Candidate's answer

(a) Opportunity cost, or alternative cost as it is also known, is the next best alternative sacrificed or given up, whenever an economic agent (for example, a producer or a consumer) makes a choice or decision.

The patient treatment frontier in Extract B, which as the accompanying text indicates is an example of a production possibility frontier, shows all the possible combinations of general practitioner and dental treatments which can be provided from available resources, given the state of technical knowledge.

Points A and B on the patient treatment frontier can be used to illustrate opportunity cost within the health service. Point A represents a situation in which approximately 45 GP services and 10 dental services are produced and made available. Because all available resources are being used (both A and B being on the frontier), a decision to increase provision of dental services to 23 (shown at point B on the frontier) would involve cutting provision of GP services to approximately 20. The opportunity cost of 13 extra dental treatments would be 25 sacrificed GP treatments. **4/4 marks** 𝓮 The candidate writes an excellent answer, displaying accurate knowledge and confident application of the opportunity cost concept, which earns all 4 marks. She has slightly over-written her answer — paragraph 2 could have been omitted.

(b) Extract A illustrates the problem of scarcity in the statement that a 'queue is a good example of a non-price rationing mechanism'. If there is no need to ration — as in the case of a free good such as air — then there is no scarcity: the good is available at zero cost and in unlimited quantity so people can consume as much as they wish without the need to pay a price. It follows that when there is a need to ration, there must be evidence of scarcity. Similar evidence of the economic problem of scarcity is provided by Extract C, which describes the need to ration scarce resources in the health service. All points on the patient treatment frontier in Extract B also illustrate the economic problem of scarcity. My earlier example explained how a decision to produce 15 extra dental treatments would require scarce resources to be diverted from the provision of GP treatments, leading to a loss of 25 GP treatments.

Extracts A and C mention queues, waiting lists, 'delay and denial', rationing-by-quantity and, of course, the price mechanism as methods of resolving the problem of excess demand. **6/6 marks**

𝓮 It is difficult to see how the candidate could improve this answer, which earns all 4 of the marks available in the mark scheme for explaining how the data illustrate the economic problem of scarcity, plus the 2 marks for identifying the various methods mentioned in the data of resolving the problem of excess demand. Wisely, with regard to the latter, the candidate sticks strictly to the instruction to 'identify', and avoids the temptation to expand unnecessarily on each of the methods she identifies.

(c) Queues and waiting lists ration the excess demand which occurs either when a good is provided 'free' at zero price, or when it is underpriced, i.e. a price is charged but it is less than the equilibrium price which would clear the market. The case for using queues and waiting lists as the main method of rationing demand within the NHS stems from the fact that health care is a merit good. A merit good such as health care ends up being under-consumed if consumers have to pay market prices to obtain the benefits of the good. By contrast, when health care is provided free, with its provision financed from taxation, under-consumption is eliminated and social welfare is increased. Further advantages are that health services are provided on the basis of need rather than the ability to pay, and the poor are not excluded as they would be in a market-based system.

However, there are disadvantages. First, people tend to undervalue services provided free by the state, as evidenced by failure to turn up for hospital and GP appointments. Second, queues and waiting lists are economically inefficient in a number of ways. Patients waste their time sitting in queues and, perhaps most importantly, some diseases such as cancer require immediate diagnosis and speedy treatment if lives are to be saved. Queues and waiting lists may mean that the treatment is received too late and that patients die unnecessarily. Third, according to Extract A, waiting lists are used in the NHS as evidence for a need to increase the resources devoted to the NHS. This implies that planners within the NHS are responding to false information signalled by the waiting lists, and that scarce resources are wasted when planners decide to increase total resources employed in the NHS to try to get rid of the excess demand. **12/15 marks**

This is nearly but not quite an excellent answer. The candidate's answer comfortably reaches Level 4 — I have awarded 12 marks, placing it at the top end of the 10–12 mark range in Level 4 — but she has provided too little evaluation of the very good 'case for' and 'case against' arguments in her answer, so she fails to reach Level 5. At times, she seems to be answering a slightly different question to the one set: namely, discussing the case for providing health care free. However, this does not seriously weaken the quality of her answer.

To reach Level 5, the candidate should have written a concluding paragraph evaluating the relative merits of her counter-arguments. She might have argued that, as queues and waiting lists are really a response to under-provision of resources in the NHS, the latter is where the deep-seated problem lies. Maybe the solution lies neither in a market-based system in which prices are charged nor in the use of queues and waiting lists as in the NHS currently. Compulsory private insurance-based systems, as used in many continental European countries, may provide health care more efficiently and equitably, avoiding the disadvantages of prices, queues and waiting lists as allocative mechanisms.

Scored 22/25   88% = grade A

Question 4 Tobacco

Total for this question: 25 marks

Study **Extracts A**, **B** and **C**, and then answer **all** parts of the question which follow.

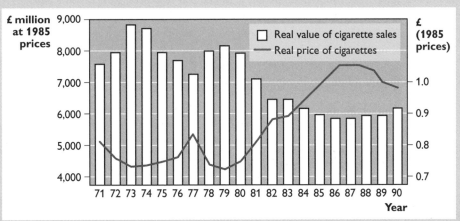

Extract A: The real value of cigarette sales and the real price of cigarettes, 1971–90

Note: all figures at constant 1985 prices.   Source: *Guardian*, 2 March 1991.

Extract B: Tobacco is a demerit good

A number of arguments can be used to justify government intervention in the free market to reduce smoking. First, tobacco is a demerit good. As with any demerit good, there are considerable external costs involved in smoking. Second, as is also the case with other demerit goods such as alcohol, the long-term costs suffered by the smoker are greater than the short-term costs. Third, as a majority of Britain's 15 million smokers are in the lowest income groups, the adverse effects of smoking are suffered more than proportionately by the poor.

Adapted from *Guardian*, 2 March 1991 and 17 May 1997.

Extract C: Tobacco advertising

The government's plan to ban cigarette advertising has sparked considerable outrage in the advertising and tobacco industries. The tobacco industry argues that consumers have a right to know about a product if it is legally on sale. The tobacco industry also claims that advertising does not increase the overall size of the market; it simply redistributes it.

ata–response question 4

> The tobacco industry's critics counter that advertising increases overall demand and makes demand less sensitive to price — or more inelastic. They also draw attention to the addictive properties of tobacco. Advertising encourages young people to start smoking. But advertising becomes less necessary once the smoker has developed the habit and has been hooked.
>
> Adapted from *Guardian*, 17 May 1997.

(a) **Compare the changes shown in Extract A in the real value of cigarette sales and the real price of cigarettes over the period shown by the data.** (4 marks)

(b) **Briefly explain, and illustrate on a supply and demand diagram, the assertion in Extract C that advertising increases overall demand for cigarettes and makes demand less sensitive to price — or more price inelastic.** (6 marks)

(c) **Evaluate the case *for* and *against* banning consumption of tobacco.** (15 marks)

■ ■ ■

Candidate's answer

(a) There was a negative or inverse relationship between the real value of cigarette sales and the real price of cigarettes over the period shown by the data. This was caused by people responding to higher cigarette prices by smoking less. An increase in the real price means that cigarette prices rose faster than inflation or the average price level of all goods measured by the Retail Price Index (RPI). The rapid rise in the real price of cigarettes was caused by the government increasing taxation on tobacco. **1/4 marks**

> 🄴 This is a classic example of a knowledgeable candidate scoring a relatively low mark by drifting away from the set question.
>
> Unfortunately, only the first sentence of the candidate's answer is relevant. This picks up 1 of the available 4 marks. To earn the other 3 marks, the candidate would need to note that although over the whole period 1971–90 the real price of cigarettes rose from just over £0.80 to just under £1.00, while the real value of sales fell from £7.5 billion to about £6.1 billion, there were three periods in the data when the real price fell and sales rose.

(b) A successful advertising campaign influences tastes and preferences favourably, causing people to demand more cigarettes at all prices. On my diagram, this shifts the demand curve for cigarettes rightwards from D_1 to D_2. If the advertising campaign makes smokers less sensitive to price (perhaps by making them more sensitive to brand image), the demand curve D_2 will also be more inelastic — a rise in cigarette prices will result in a less than proportionate fall in demand. Steep demand curves are inelastic.

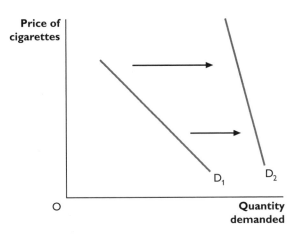

6/6 marks

The candidate has written a very good answer to this question, earning all 6 marks. His diagram is accurate and clearly labelled, and his explanation shows a good understanding of demand theory and elasticity of demand.

Remember, however, not to confuse *slope* and *elasticity*, which the candidate may be doing. Elasticity varies from point to point moving down a demand curve such as D_1 or D_2.

(c) The case for banning the consumption of tobacco stems from the fact that most people regard tobacco as a demerit good. The state believes that consumption of demerit goods harms people and is an example of market failure. The state sees itself as a better judge of what is in people's interest than the people themselves. Therefore the state believes it is justified in limiting people's freedom of choice in order to correct the market failure represented by the demerit good. Hence the case for banning consumption of tobacco.

The case against banning consumption of tobacco is that 'people rather than the government know best' as to what is in their self-interest. Banning tobacco consumption is an example of the 'nanny state'; it is undemocratic and it may lead to totalitarianism and dictatorship.

I personally believe that consumption of tobacco should not be banned but that advertising of tobacco should be banned. This would reduce the possibility that people, particularly teenagers, would start smoking and become addicted because they were influenced by the fact that tobacco advertisements associate smoking with glamour and personal success. **10/15 marks**

Wisely, the candidate obeys the instruction to 'evaluate the case for and against' and finishes his answer by concluding that in his view the case against is stronger.

Because of sound structure and a conclusion, rather than strength of content, the answer just reaches Level 4 (10–12 marks), earning 10 of the available 15 marks. The candidate starts his answer by explaining clearly why tobacco is a

data-response question 4

demerit good. He then provides one 'case for banning' and one 'case against banning' argument. Both arguments are valid and earn some credit, but neither is fully explained. To reach Level 5, the candidate needs to develop both of his arguments and/or to include at least one other 'case for' and 'case against' argument. The obvious way to develop the 'case for' argument is to explain how, when markets provide tobacco, over-consumption occurs and third parties are adversely affected by the negative externalities associated with smoking. His answer would benefit from more economics and less political theory.

Scored 17/25   68% = grade B

Question 5 Economies of scale

Total for this question: 25 marks

Study **Extracts A**, **B** and **C**, and then answer **all** parts of the question which follow.

Extract A: The bigger the better?

Firms seek to get bigger. As markets globalise, the argument goes, there will be room only for a handful of huge international companies selling global brands. The bigger a company is, the more efficient it will be. So unless management can get it to be the number one or two it will lack the economies of scale to be competitive.

In fact, over the last decade, in more than 80% of markets, the largest companies have not generated the highest profits for shareholders, who have generally done better buying into smaller competitors. The winners have not been the biggest — Boeing, GM, IBM, Procter & Gamble. It has been their smaller competitors — General Dynamics, Dell and Colgate — which have produced the better financial results.

Adapted from an article by Peter Doyle, Professor of Marketing and Strategic Management at the University of Warwick Business School, Guardian, 27 May 2000.

Extract B: The oil transportation industry

In the oil transportation industry, the larger the tanker, the greater the economies of scale. But very large super-tankers cannot enter shallow ports. A wider tanker with a shallow draught does not yield as many economies of scale as a conventional super-tanker, but it is more efficient than a conventional small tanker.

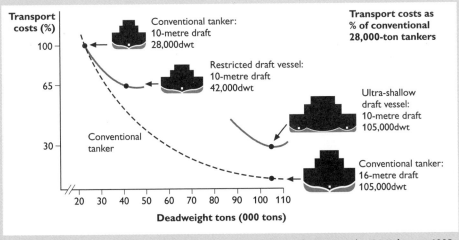

Source: The Economist, 20 February 1982.

data–response question 5

Extract C: Big can be bad

Big companies may reap economies of scale, but when competition is limited and monopoly power is great, they are unlikely to pass them on to consumers. When markets are dominated by big companies, there is less opportunity for small ones to emerge.

Major companies get what they want. The bigger they become, the more power they accumulate to influence governments to act in their interest. As they grow, their concerns become ever further removed from those of the citizens they dwarf, until the world is run not for the benefit of its 6 billion poor or merely comfortable inhabitants, but for that of a handful of perverse billionaires. Glaxo-Wellcome has already tried to bully the NHS into buying its anti-flu drug; the bigger company to which it now belongs could start to shape national health policies to suit itself. When businesses dine on each other, the rest of us get swallowed.

Adapted from an article by George Monbiot, *Guardian*, 20 January 2000.

(a) Extract A states: 'The bigger a company is, the more efficient it will be.'
Explain *one* meaning of the term 'efficiency' in economics. (4 marks)

(b) Briefly describe the type of economy of scale illustrated in Extract B, *and* explain how the extract illustrates limitations to the economies of scale that can be achieved in the oil transportation industry. (6 marks)

(c) In the light of the information in the data, discuss the case *for* and *against* governments intervening to prevent big firms growing even larger. (15 marks)

■ ■ ■

Candidate's answer

(a) Productive efficiency is the efficiency concept I shall define. There are two ways of defining productive efficiency. Firstly, a firm is productively efficient if it produces its chosen level of output at the lowest possible cost. Secondly, all points on a production possibility frontier are productively efficient. **4/4 marks**

> *e* The candidate has written an excellent answer, which earns all 4 marks. While she correctly notes that there are two ways of defining productive efficiency, she would still have earned full marks had she restricted her answer to just one of these.
>
> The AS specification requires that you show knowledge and understanding of two types of economic efficiency: productive and allocative efficiency. Full marks could therefore be earned by defining allocative efficiency. The specification defines allocative efficiency as occurring 'when the goods and services produced match people's needs and preferences'. See p. 32 for a fuller definition of allocative efficiency.

(b) The diagram in Extract B shows a type of economy of scale known as 'volume economies of scale' or 'economies of increased dimensions'. In the case of the oil tankers shown in the diagram, volume economies mean that when the size of a tanker is increased from, say, 28,000 tons to 105,000 tons, the amount of oil that the tanker can carry increases more than proportionately. The cost of transporting each unit of oil therefore falls.

However, the diagram also shows that larger tankers are less flexible or more difficult to use than small tankers. Small tankers can enter many more ports because in some ports large tankers would run aground due to the shallow water. This limits the usefulness of 'super-tankers' and the ability to exploit full economies of scale in the oil transportation industry. **6/6 marks**

e Another excellent answer, earning all 6 marks. The candidate correctly identifies the type of economy of scale that is illustrated in Extract B. Volume economies are a type of 'technical economy of scale', other forms being managerial, marketing and financial economies of scale. Technical economies — including volume economies — are so called because they result from the technical nature of production, i.e. the way in which the firm employs its capital (machinery and plant) as it increases the scale of productive capacity.

Returning to volume economies of scale, with many types of capital equipment (e.g. metal smelters, transport containers, storage tanks and warehouses), costs increase less rapidly than capacity. When a storage tank or boiler is doubled in dimension, its storage capacity actually increases eightfold. And since heat loss depends on the area of the container's walls (which will have increased only fourfold) and not upon volume, a large smelter or boiler is technically more efficient than a small one.

(c) Governments intervene in markets to prevent large firms growing even larger because they believe that large firms may misuse their market power. In an extreme case, the firm may become a monopoly, i.e. the only firm in the market. Monopolies can be bad for a number of reasons. Because a monopoly faces no competition, it may incur high costs of production and face little pressure to reduce costs. In other words, monopolies may be productively inefficient. Monopolies are also quite likely to be allocatively inefficient, i.e. not producing the goods consumers want.

Whereas competitive markets are characterised by 'consumer sovereignty' (producing goods consumers want, with the 'consumer as king'), highly concentrated markets with just one or a few large firms exhibit 'producer sovereignty'. In effect, the monopolist says to consumers 'take it or leave it'. Monopolists may restrict consumer choice by producing only a narrow range of goods. Lack of competition may also reduce the incentive to innovate or to produce better quality goods in order to please customers.

Large firms are not, however, always bad. Some markets are so large that even if a particular firm grows very large, there are still lots of other firms and plenty of competition in the market. In such a market, there is no need for the government to intervene to prevent the growth of large firms. Indeed, the government may actually encourage the growth of large firms in order to promote economies of scale. **12/15 marks**

e This answer is again excellent — but in this case, only not quite perfect. More often than not, the last part of a Unit 1: Markets and Market Failure data–response question asks for a discussion of a two-sided issue. To reach a high Level 5, the answer *must* discuss both the 'case for' and the 'case against' in sufficient depth, before coming to a reasoned conclusion. The trouble with this candidate's answer is the lack of balance. She writes a brilliant 'case for' government intervention, and if she could maintain the same quality in the rest of her answer, she would obtain full marks. Unfortunately, the rest of her answer is much too cursory. She makes one good 'case against' argument, relating to the overall size of the market. She might have developed this argument by relating the domestic market to the world market. Imports increase competition when there is only one UK-based firm. Likewise, she should have developed her brief statement of economies of scale. Finally, she might have argued that far from preferring an 'easy life', monopolies may be innovative.

The candidate just about includes a conclusion in her answer, implying that the government should consider each example of a growing firm on its merits before deciding whether to prevent further growth. However, this conclusion is not firmly made. Nevertheless, because the candidate included one 'case against' argument and briefly mentioned economies of scale, overall her answer just reaches a high Level 4 standard, earning 12 of the available 15 marks.

Scored 22/25   88% = grade A

Question 6

Specialisation and the division of labour

Total for this question: 25 marks

Study **Extracts A**, **B** and **C**, and then answer **all** parts of the question which follow.

Extract A: Specialisation and factors of production

A country's advantage in producing and hence selling certain products stems in part from its endowments of economic resources. If a country is well endowed with capital relative to labour, such as we would expect in an industrialised country, then it would be expected that the country would have an advantage in producing goods that use large amounts of capital relative to labour and selling them abroad at competitive prices.

The country's advantage in capital-intensive rather than labour-intensive goods would lead it to export capital-intensive goods and import labour-intensive goods. In this way, the country would be utilising its relative abundance of capital and economising on its relative shortage of labour.

Adapted from *Exchange and Patterns of Trade*, published by The Open University, 1985.

Extract B: Globalisation and the division of labour

A globally integrated economy can lead to a better division of labour between countries, allowing low-wage countries to specialise in labour-intensive tasks while high-wage countries use workers in more productive ways. It will allow firms to exploit bigger economies of scale. And with globalisation, capital can be shifted to whatever country offers the most productive investment opportunities, not trapped at home financing projects with poor returns.

Critics of globalisation take a gloomier view. They predict that increased competition from low-wage developing countries will destroy jobs and push down wages in today's rich economies. There will be a 'race to the bottom' as countries reduce wages, taxes, welfare benefits and environmental controls to make themselves more 'competitive'. Pressure to compete will erode the ability of governments to set their own economic policies.

Adapted from *The Economist*, 18 October 1997.

data–response question 6

Extract C: Putting General Motors' 'world car' together

Production of motor vehicle parts is so internationally dispersed that major manufacturers produce 'world cars' from components made in factories scattered throughout the world.

Source: *Financial Times*, 26 August 1981.

(a) Explain the meaning of the terms 'economic resources' *and* 'capital-intensive' which are mentioned in Extract A. (4 marks)

(b) Explain how Extract C illustrates the division of labour between countries. (6 marks)

(c) Discuss how the international division of labour may affect the economic problem of scarcity *and* whether, in your view, the advantages of this division of labour exceed any disadvantages. (15 marks)

■ ■ ■

Candidate's answer

(a) 'Economic resources' are also known as factors of production. They comprise both renewable and non-renewable resources. There are four factors of production: (i) land, which includes natural resources such as rain forests, a naturally fertile soil and minerals in the earth's crust; (ii) labour, the workforce of the economy; (iii) capital (manufactured stocks of resources); and (iv) entrepreneurship, or the business men and women who organise production and take risks.

'Capital-intensive' goods are those whose production relies more on the use of capital than on labour, i.e. a lot of machinery and relatively little labour is used to produce goods. **4/4 marks** *e* The marking scheme for this question allows 2 marks to be earned for an accurate explanation of each of the terms. In this case, the candidate earns 2 marks for his explanation of 'economic resources' and 2 marks for the explanation of 'capital-intensive', thereby achieving full marks. He writes just enough for full marks, and avoids the trap that many students fall into of writing too much in his answer to part (a) simply because it is the first part of the question.

(b) Extract C illustrates the division of labour between countries because it shows how the components of one good (an automobile) are manufactured in factories scattered throughout the world. It shows how the firm GM, which markets cars under the Vauxhall brand name in Britain, is actively adopting 'globalisation' as it exploits bigger economies of scale and draws on the benefits of size in different continents. General Motors is using specialist production techniques to make it more cost effective to produce a car than if all production were taking place in one country. **3/6 marks**

e Because of the candidate's failure to make sufficient use of the information provided by Extract C, his answer earns 3 of the available 6 marks. The answer picks up 3 marks for showing an understanding of the meaning of the international division of labour, and for limited use of the information in Extract C. But unfortunately, the candidate makes no use of the information provided by the *direction of flow of the arrows* in Extract C. He displays his knowledge of globalisation and economies of scale. This is largely irrelevant for this question. The knowledge would be better applied to part (c).

(c) The economic problem of scarcity is basically that resources have to be allocated between competing uses because wants are infinite while resources, which provide the means of gratifying these wants, are scarce. Scarcity means that choices have to be made about the use of resources.

The division of labour increases labour productivity so more output is produced. When applied internationally or between countries, the division of labour leads to a more efficient allocation of resources in the world economy as the most efficient methods of production available in the world are used to produce goods or parts of goods. This means that more of the 'infinite wants' can be satisfied.

There are several advantages and disadvantages of the division of labour, but the advantages clearly outweigh the disadvantages. Extract B tells us that critics of the division of labour and globalisation predict that increased competition from low-paid developing countries will 'destroy jobs and push down wages in today's rich economies'. There will be a 'race to the bottom', so to speak, and eventually pressure to compete will greatly hinder the ability of governments to set their own economic policies. Also, if jobs are divided up too much, the work can become tedious and monotonous which would result in poor workmanship and reduced output per worker. Over-specialisation can lead to one country becoming overdependent on one good (e.g. Ghana and cocoa). Lower international prices or a poor harvest will reduce incomes, create unemployment and play havoc with long-term planning (e.g. shipyard,

data–response question 6

steel and textile workers are particularly affected). Another problem is that a breakdown in part of the chain of production can cause chaos within the system.

However, the advantages exceed the disadvantages. Extract B tells us that the division of labour allows firms to 'exploit bigger economies of scale' which would in turn benefit the consumer. Extract A informs us that countries would be able to exploit and use their economic resources more effectively and efficiently. A specialised worker is more efficient than a 'jack of all trades'. It also makes it cost-effective to provide workers with specialist tools. Time is saved because a worker is not constantly changing tasks, moving around from place to place. Workers can also specialise in those trades in which they are best suited. Thus the advantages of the division of labour exceed the disadvantages. **10/15 marks**

I have placed the candidate's answer at the bottom of the 10–12-mark range for the Level 4 standard. He answers the 'lower-order' part of the question very well, neatly stating the economic problem of scarcity and convincingly explaining why greater international division of labour might lessen the problem. My only slight quibble with this part of his answer is that he mentions efficiency twice without explaining explicitly the meaning he attaches to this very important economic term.

To reach Level 5 and grade A overall for the question, the candidate would have to develop rather more his discussion of the advantages and disadvantages of the international division of labour and provide more justification of his conclusion that the advantages exceed the disadvantages.

Too much of the candidate's discussion relates to advantages and disadvantages more relevant to the division of labour within a particular workplace than to the international division of labour (namely, his discussion of tedium and monotony and his 'jack of all trades' analogy). The candidate also relies too much on copying out from the extracts without imposing his own stamp on the information copied out.

Scored 17/25   68% = grade B